J
613.7
Mon

Monroe, Judy.

Understanding weight-
loss programs

A Teen
Eating Disorder
Prevention
Book

Understanding Weight-Loss Programs

Judy Monroe

The Rosen Publishing Group, Inc./New York

Published in 1999 by The Rosen Publishing Group, Inc.
29 East 21st Street, New York, NY 10010

Library of Congress Cataloging-in-Publication Data

Monroe, Judy.
Understanding Weight-Loss Programs / Judy Monroe.
p. cm. — (A teen eating disorder prevention book)
Includes bibliographical references and index.
Summary: Discusses the weight-loss industry including why this business is thriving, the many products and services offered, and the pros and cons of various weight-loss methods.
ISBN 0-8239-2866-7
1. Weight loss—Juvenile literature. 2. Reducing diets—Juvenile literature. 3. Eating disorders—Juvenile literature. 4. Eating disorders in adolescence—Juvenile literature. [1. Weight loss. 2. Reducing diets. 3. Eating disorders.] I. Title. II. Title: Understanding weight loss programs. III. Series.
RM222.2M563 1999
613.7—dc21

99-23313
CIP

Manufactured in the United States of America

ABOUT THE AUTHOR

Judy Monroe, M.A., M.P.H., has written numerous books and magazine articles for teens on health issues.

Contents

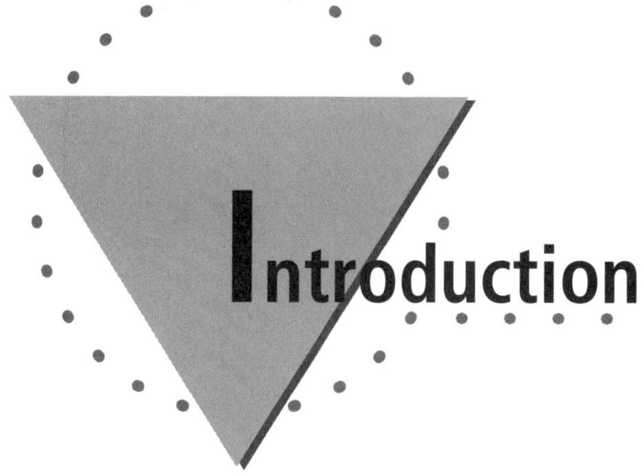

Introduction

"More money gone to waste," Maida sighed, tossing the book she was reading onto the floor. "You know, I've read at least eight different diet books and tried just about every one of their diets—and not one of them has worked. And look at you! I mean, you're skinny as a rail! What exactly are you doing?"

Jenny laughed. "Well, it took me a few tries to find something. Remember that rubber suit I had for a while?"

"Yeah," Maida smiled. "That was the craziest thing!"

"It was supposed to 'melt away the pounds,'" Jenny said. "But all I got out of it was a nasty rash. How was I to know I was allergic to whatever was in that thing?"

"But you found something?" Maida asked.

Jenny pulled a small box out of her jeans pocket. "Here's what I found. These pills do the trick for me. I get them at the drugstore.

I don't even need a prescription for them."

"What are those? Diet pills?" Maida asked.

"Yes," Jenny replied.

"But don't they cause problems? I heard they're not good."

"C'mon, Maida. How bad could they be? Besides, would you rather be fat?"

Maida looked at the pills and shrugged her shoulders. She picked up a colorful brochure from the floor next to her and waved it in the air. "Hey, Jen! Listen to this!" Maida exclaimed. "You know what I'm gonna try next? There's this weight-loss center down at the strip mall. I've been reading their ad. It's got simply everything! Their weight-loss program sounds ***fabulous****!"*

CONFUSING WEIGHT-LOSS CLAIMS

Maida and Jenny are looking for a quick and easy way to lose weight. So are an estimated 65 million other Americans. They have tried many different ways to reach their goal. Some, like Maida, opt for commercial weight-loss programs, books, tapes, or videos. Jenny has tried weight-loss gadgets and gizmos. Diet pills, powders, or liquids appeal to others.

Trying to sort through all the weight-loss claims can be confusing and costly. Many are often misleading, unproven, or just plain false. But most people are seldom armed with facts about weight-loss claims. They would find it hard to answer these questions:

- How do you determine which weight-loss program or plan is best for you?

- Do any of them work? New diets seem to pop up every week.
- Do any of the weight-loss pills, liquids, gadgets, and creams really work?
- Are there any safe ways to lose weight and keep it off permanently?

PROMISES, PROMISES

While many weight-loss programs, diets, and gizmos lure people with the promise of a slim, attractive body, the results seldom measure up. Most are not successful. In fact, the Federal Trade Commission (FTC) says this: While some people will take off weight by using weight-loss programs and products, few—perhaps 5 percent—will manage to keep all of it off in the long run.

According to medical research, ninety percent of all dieters regain some or all of the weight originally lost. At least one-third gain more. An increasing amount of research has confirmed these failure rates. Research also has found that genetic and physiological factors play important roles in determining body size.

Some people like Maida and Jenny do not need to lose weight. Both teens are at a healthy weight for their height and body shape. Yet, like many American teens, they think they need to be thin. They obsess about being thin because thinness seems to equal success, popularity, and happiness.

Their beauty ideals are everywhere: ultra-thin fashion models, beauty pageant winners, and TV and movie stars. However, these women generally do not have typical or even healthy female figures. No matter how hard they try, the vast majority of females will never be able to mold their bodies to a model's dimensions.

DIETING HARM

According to Frances M. Berg, editor of *Healthy Weight Journal,* weight issues have become an obsession in the United States. In her book, *Afraid to Eat,* she gives some alarming statistics about this obsession:

- More than two-thirds of high school girls are dieting.
- Twenty-five percent of high school boys are dieting.
- Twenty percent of high school girls take diet pills.
- More than 50 percent of teen girls are undernourished.
- Many female and male teens are using laxatives, diuretics, fasting, and vomiting to slim down.

The quest to be thin can sometimes lead to serious physical and psychological consequences and problems. About 10 percent of teens in the United States, mostly females, suffer from harmful eating disorders. Someone who suffers from an eating disorder constantly thinks about food, weight, and dieting. Family, friends, hobbies, and healthy activities fade in importance. An eating disorder can lead to serious physical and mental health problems and can even cause death.

WHAT YOU WILL FIND IN THIS BOOK

This book will explore the weight-loss industry, including:

- Why this huge business is booming
- Its many products and services
- The pros and cons of various weight-loss methods

It will provide you with the facts behind the appealing weight-loss claims so that you can make wise choices. In addition, you will learn how to spot and avoid outright scams and fake products and services.

You will learn about the unhealthy aspects of dieting and will be encouraged to consider thoroughly the costs and consequences of the dieting decisions you make. You will find out that there is no set weight for each person, but that there are guidelines on looking good and feeling good about yourself. This book explores what a healthy weight is, and what a healthy weight means for you.

1 The Weight-Loss Industry

Mai has tried dozens of diets. She says, "Once I went on a 400-calorie-a-day liquid diet. One of my friends had read about it in a magazine, so we tried it. I was so hungry after two days that I started shoveling everything I could into my mouth until I thought I'd explode."

Mai's most painful diet was an all-fruit program. "I ate oranges and grapefruits until I had sores in my mouth," she recalled. Over the years, she's collected two shelves of diet books. Each one promises a surefire plan for shedding extra pounds. But nothing Mai has tried has ever led to permanent weight loss.

Every year, millions of teens like Mai go on diets to meet some goal of being thin. Some diet to be more popular with peers or the opposite sex. Some do it to improve their athletic abilities or to meet weight requirements for a sport. Others diet to prove that they are in control of their own life.

Dieting will help some teens lose, but not in the way that they hope. Most teens don't need to diet in the first place, because they are not overweight. Even if they diet, most won't lose the weight they want to—at least not for the long run. Dieting has proven to be one of the worst ways to get your body in shape. It can lead to an endless cycle of dieting, losing weight, ending a diet, gaining weight back, feeling frustrated and angry—and dieting again.

This pattern produces many negative results. Dieting interferes with normal metabolism, or the rate at which the body burns food. It sets up an unhealthy attitude toward eating, which can lead to depression, anxiety, and other mental health problems. And it doesn't give you what you want—a permanently thin body.

A BIG BUSINESS

Each day, approximately 65 million Americans are dieting. That means one out of every two adults is on a diet at any given time. Although most dieters are female teens and adults, more and more teen and adult males are trying to lose weight.

Many dieters think that they need to buy something—diet products, plans, or membership in a program—to lose weight. They have many options from which to choose. These range from self-help books, to companies that combine nutritional counseling with the sale of their own low-calorie food products, to medical providers who offer a comprehensive approach to weight reduction.

Over 17,000 diet plans, programs, and products

exist today. New ones pop up all the time. Ever hopeful, dieters are willing to spend money over and over again on seemingly new, slickly marketed diet products and programs.

Losing weight is hard for most people. That's why they often turn to various weight-loss methods to help them shed some pounds. With so many people trying to lose weight, the weight-loss industry pulls in big money. According to Marketdata, a market research firm in Tampa, Florida, the American weight-loss industry generates sales of $35 billion each year. The weight-loss business outside the United States may be just as profitable.

THE LURE OF THIN

Why are so many teens buying into the promise of quick, easy weight loss? And why the emphasis on thinness? In America being thin is what's in. Health experts report that from one-half to two-thirds of all teen girls and nearly one-quarter of all teen boys see themselves as overweight. As a result, many are trying to lose weight by using various ineffective and possibly unsafe methods.

Pressure to lose weight and be thin is increasing. And there are so many contributing factors—pressure from peers, from parents, and from the media. But the truth is that most teens are not overweight. Nor are they fat. Medical doctors find that less than one in five teen girls is actually overweight. Instead, many teens have unrealistic ideas about a healthy weight that works for their height and body type.

The pressure to be thin is often linked with peer pressure. Most teens want to fit in and be accepted

Weight-Loss Method	Description
Weight-loss centers or commercial diet services or programs	Includes Weight Watchers, Jenny Craig, Nutri/System, and many others. Most centers provide diets. Some also provide various products and services such as exercise plans, weight-loss drugs, dietary supplements, books, videos, counseling, and so on.
Diet plans	Found in diet books and articles in magazines. There are many different types of plans: low-calorie, high-fat, low-fat, high-carbohydrate, low-carbohydrate, special foods, liquids, raw foods, and so on.
Drugs or diet supplements (often in the form of pills, capsules, tablets)	This includes nonprescription drugs such as laxatives, diuretics, and diet supplements that

Drugs or supplements (continued)	claim to speed metabolism, suppress appetite, or block digestion. Also includes prescription drugs like fen-phen, herbs, fat "blockers," and bulk producers or fillers.
Diet devices and gadgets	Appetite-suppressing eyeglasses, weight-loss earrings, gum, soaps, body wraps, breath spray, weight-loss clothing, reducing creams, and so forth.
Exercise	Passive exercise tables, electrical muscle stimulators, excessive exercise.
Hypnotism	Individual or group.
Purging, vomiting, fasting	Dangerous ways to eliminate food.
Surgery	Gastric bypass, liposuction, tummy tuck, jaw wiring, gastric balloon.

by their peers. Many think that they have to be thin to be attractive and popular. Not only that, but teens are constantly getting pummeled with messages to be thin from the media.

Karen, fifteen, says that teen magazines are a big thing with her and her friends. "There are always articles on how to become thinner and sexier and how to be attractive to boys," she says. "Every issue has something—the latest makeup, the coolest clothing, the hottest shoes, and lots of other stuff. It's like you keep getting the message that to get a boyfriend, to get a boy to even ***notice*** *you, you need to smell good, dress right, look right, and be thin like a model. Sometimes I've even sent away for the diet and weight-loss products that are in the magazines. There are lots of them, like in the back pages, in the mail-order section. I mean, I want to have a boyfriend—and I know the best way to attract someone is to have a fine body. Like thin, firm, and with a small waist."*

Sometimes parents pressure their kids about how they should look. As a child, Jolene was short and solidly built. She wasn't heavy. But her dad thought she was. Jolene remembered:

"My dad used to call me fat. All the time. Like a joke. I don't think he meant it to hurt me, but it sure did. I mean, I barely saw him because he worked so much. No matter what I did to attract his attention, I couldn't seem to get him to notice me. And it wasn't like I was

just sitting around, vegetating—I was very active as a teenager, and I used to play soccer, kickball, and softball with the kids in the neighborhood after school and on the weekends. And I thought I was okay-looking. But Dad wanted me to look . . . different. He wanted me to be beautiful, like a model, and thin. I think he saw me as a kind of reflection of himself—the more perfect I was, the more perfect **he** *was. And I guess I just got tired of it. I got tired of his jokes and the way he just kind of ignored me, and so one time I pretty much stopped eating. Period. I drank lots of fruit juice. And I went for three days like that, starving myself, before I gave up on my crazy diet plan. Dad, of course, never noticed any difference."*

As if peer pressure and parental pressure weren't enough, the media hammers the thin message home. It bombards us with all kinds of messages, playing up the image that thin people are healthier and more successful, popular, and attractive. Good things in life are pictured as happening only to thin people. In contrast, overweight people are seen as lazy or lacking self-control. Teens see and hear these common messages constantly in magazines, newspapers, advertisements, movies, and television sitcoms.

The fashion and cosmetics industries contribute to the bombardment of thin images in the media. Advertising campaigns for fashion and beauty products often target teens and preteens. These industries know that these two groups spend a lot of their parents' (and their own) money on fashion, beauty, entertainment, and leisure products. Many fashion and body products promote body insecurity. Think of all the ads you've seen that ask teen viewers: "Do you have pimples?" "Is your hair limp and does it need body?" "Are you overweight?" "Do you have body odor?" If you can answer "yes" to any of these questions, then you can be sure that there are lots of products out there on the market to help you take care of your "problem"!

A constant stream of advertising delivers the same message over and over again: **"Thin is in."** Hearing and seeing the same message repeatedly, many people start to believe it. Over time thin messages can distort the way most people view themselves and others.

The issue of good health creates another pressure to be thin. Some researchers say that being overweight can cause premature death. In America obesity-related disorders claim about 300,000 lives each year. This results in a whopping $100 billion in medical costs!

When teens buy in to an unrealistic weight or body image, then losing weight becomes an important, ongoing quest. Many turn to the weight-loss industry for fast fixes. There are plenty of methods to choose from, and most promise fast, easy weight-loss results. But the promises seldom measure up to the desired result.

LOW SUCCESS RATES

No matter what weight-loss method is used, most people manage to take off some weight. But few keep all of it off for long. One reason for the low success rate is that many people look for quick and easy solutions to weight loss. They find it hard to believe that in this age of scientific advances and medical miracles, an effortless weight-loss method doesn't exist. When one product or service doesn't keep weight off, people rush to buy another equally useless weight-loss item or service.

What many people don't know is that the weight-loss industry lacks quality control. This means that all too often, no scientific evidence whatsoever exists to support the claims of the various weight-loss programs and products. So the real winners in the weight-loss business are the makers and sellers of questionable weight-loss programs and products. They pocket large profits because people continue to believe that there's an easy way to melt off the pounds.

BOGUS CLAIMS

"You really think this'll work?" Laura asked, pointing to the can on the supermarket shelf.

"Of course it'll work," Shaun said, grabbing can after can and loading them into his shopping cart. "It's a diet shake, for crying out loud."

Laura scratched her chin. "But how can you be sure?"

Shaun gave her an "oh, please" sort of look, and held a can up to her face.

"C'mon, Laura. Look at the can. Look at the ad." He held up a colorful flier for her to see. "The ad says it's a diet shake. A guaranteed fat burner. And you know, ads have to be true or the manufacturer couldn't say that stuff."

Wrong, wrong, wrong.

Like Shaun, many people believe that weight-loss products, gizmos, programs, or plans are screened or tested by medical professionals, and that only the ones that work can be advertised and sold.

Every year Americans waste huge amounts of money on bogus weight-loss products and services. Most weight-loss advertising is aimed at people's fear of being unattractive. Misleading ads for weight-loss products and services can be found in magazines, newspapers, and mail-order catalogs, on television and radio, or via telemarketing and the Internet. They also appear in drugstores, supermarkets, and health food stores. You may have seen weight-loss ads tacked to telephone polls or slipped under the windshield wipers of cars in a parking lot.

Some products are sold by direct mail. Weight-loss sellers use subscriber lists from magazines and other sources to put together their own mailing lists. Many direct mail ads are for weight-reduction schemes. Sometimes the direct mail ads for fake products look like authentic reproductions of newspaper articles. Usually, though, they have never been published. To pull in the reader, the reproductions are accompanied by a handwritten note in the margin or on a Post-It. A typical note might read, "Dear Linda, This really works! Try it. J."

THE LAW

Who protects people from bogus weight-loss products and services? Three federal agencies and various state and local agencies can enforce laws against fake health products and services: the Food and Drug Administration (FDA), the Federal Trade Commission (FTC), and the U.S. Postal Service.

Unfortunately the weight-loss business is just too big for these three agencies to keep track of every new weight-reduction service and product that comes along.

CONSUMERS BEWARE

In general the federal government doesn't test, check, or certify most companies that market weight-loss programs. One needn't be licensed, educated, or certified to run a weight-loss business or to make and sell weight-loss products. The success of a weight-loss company depends mostly on how well it markets and sells its wares. Whether the program or products actually work and are safe is seldom questioned.

Consumers, then, are pretty much on their own when trying weight-loss products and services. And that brings up another problem. Most people don't know where to get useful, objective information. They rarely have reliable tools to help them sort through the vast array of weight-loss options.

DIETING DANGERS

As the bell for morning homeroom rang, Jodi turned around to talk to Aimee. Right away, she noticed her friend's pearl earrings. "Hey," Jodi said, "you got your ears pierced!"

"Nope," Aimee smiled. "These are special

Federal Agency	What the Agency Handles
Food and Drug Administration (FDA)	Stops false and misleading labeling of foods, drugs, medical devices, and cosmetics. (Labeling includes both the information on a product's container and promotional materials.)
Federal Trade Commission (FTC)	Runs a small monitoring operation to catch and stop misleading or fake ads for foods, nonprescription drugs, cosmetics, and services. Has a very effective law, but can handle only a small percentage of the fake ads it finds.
U.S. Postal Service	Has an active program to detect and stop the sale of bogus health products through the mail. Pursues cases that might generate a large amount of mail or that could cause physical harm to the public.

earrings. They don't have posts, see? Magnets keep the two pieces on my earlobe."

"That's kinda cool," Jodi said.

"Actually," Aimee continued, "I bought them because they're suppose to control my appetite and cravings. The ad said they've been helping people lose weight for years. All I have to do is wear them every day for six to eight hours. And they only cost twenty dollars."

"Wow! Where'd you get them? I'd like to try them!"

Aimee wrote down the name and address of the company that made the earrings on a piece of paper and slipped it to Jodi.

Aimee and Jodi met up again later that day, this time in art class. Right away, Jodi noticed something wrong with Aimee. Her eyes were watery, and her ears were a fiery red.

Jodi asked, "Aimee, are you feeling okay? Why are your ears so red?"

"It was the earrings," Aimee said. "Stupid things. I threw them away, they pinched and hurt so bad." Aimee giggled. "But I guess they sort of worked . . . because while I was wearing them, the pain was so bad I couldn't think about anything else. I guess that'll keep you away from food!"

At first glance, the only thing Aimee lost was some money on worthless weight-loss earrings. Aside from being costly, weight-loss products can sometimes produce unwanted side effects or can harm the body. Luckily for Aimee, her ears stopped hurting by the next day.

Chronic or ongoing dieting can stop teens from growing to full height by affecting bone growth. Other negative effects of dieting include feeling like a failure, a drop in self-esteem, mood swings, fatigue, having trouble concentrating, becoming easily distracted, and an increasing chance of developing an eating disorder.

WEIGHT RECYCLING OR YO-YO DIETING

Kennard, seventeen, was the star forward on his high school basketball team. But when he broke his leg during practice at the beginning of the season, he began to gain weight.

"I felt so down," Kennard said, "when my doctor told me I was absolutely out for the rest of the season. Without basketball, I wasn't able to get much exercise. And because I was feeling bad, I was eating everything in sight. One day I looked in the mirror and thought: Wow . . . where'd that belly come from? And when I stepped on the bathroom scale, I realized that I had put on twenty-five pounds. So I started dieting. And with each diet I tried, I'd go along just fine for two or three weeks. But each time, the same thing happened. I'd lose like five pounds and then, one morning, I'd wake up so hungry that I'd eat everything in sight. I kept losing and gaining the same weight."

Kennard is a weight recycler, or yo-yo dieter. Weight recycling—the cycle of losing and regaining, losing and regaining—is generally the result of following one weight-loss plan or program after another. According to medical studies, weight recycling increases the chance of mental and physical health problems. In addition, weight recycling can make weight management tougher. Repeatedly losing and gaining weight can lead to a slower metabolic rate, which means that the body burns calories more slowly. It can also lead to eating disorders; poor self-esteem; feelings of failure and frustration, and an increased risk of heart disease and some forms of cancer.

As the cycle repeats itself, dieters need fewer and fewer calories to maintain their weight. This makes it harder to lose weight. The endless cycle of failure-success-failure negatively affects a person's attitude, too, often reinforcing feelings of low self-esteem.

TEENS AND THE WEIGHT-LOSS INDUSTRY

The multibillion dollar weight-loss industry has many teen customers. However, many teens are not realistic about their weight and see themselves as overweight. Teen girls generally use dieting as their main method to slim down. Teen boys tend to turn to exercise, although more are dieting these days.

A teen's quest to be thin can lead to trying fad diets, weight-loss programs, and weight-reduction products. These methods often fail to take off and maintain weight loss. Sometimes they are dangerous. Dieting is particularly risky for teens because they need varied, balanced, and nourishing food for growth and energy.

2 The Quest to Lose Weight

Starina held up a small jar. "Hey Cyndy, check this out."

"What is it?" Cyndy asked, looking at the jar's label. "Oh, it's a cream—for weight loss? This stuff says it smooths away fat."

Starina smiled. "That's why I bought it. You just rub the cream on wherever you want to get rid of fat, and the fat dissolves."

"Like magic, your fat dissolves," Cyndy read from the jar's label. "Hey, Star, I hope you haven't opened that jar yet."

Starina's smile disappeared. "I haven't. Why?"

Cyndy shook her head. "So you can return it and get your money back. That stuff's not gonna work, Star. I just read in a magazine article how people have tried to come up with weight-reduction creams for hundreds of years. But they've all been useless. There's no magic—they just don't work."

LOSING THROUGH THE AGES

People have tried various methods to lose weight for thousands of years. Back in ancient Rome, women dieted to stay slender. For those who could afford it, excess fat was removed by surgery. And, by the sixteenth century, people could buy "fat dissolving" creams, just like Starina. But it wasn't until 1830 that diet plans began to pop up in the United States, England, and France. Many of these diet plans were downright dangerous. One young girl was so worried about becoming fat that she came up with her own diet plan—one glass of vinegar a day. She died two months later from starvation.

By the middle of the 1800s, even more Americans sought weight reduction through dieting. Sometimes doctors tried to help those who wanted to lose weight by prescribing arsenic and strychnine. We now know that both substances are deadly poisons.

From the late 1800s on, newspapers and magazines contained numerous weight-reducing advertisements. "Weigh what you should weigh!" shouted one ad in 1896. "Get rid of fat," promised another.

Some of the early diet aids were dangerous; they contained strong laxatives or poisons. Others simply didn't work. They were actually made of lemonade, baking soda, or salts. But the number of fake diet aids continued to swell. In 1914 *Good Housekeeping* even published an article titled "Swindled Getting Slim." The authors warned that phony diet aids were misleading and that they did not work.

Yet, up until the turn of the century, most

Americans applauded plumpness. People felt proud if they could afford to eat as much food as they wanted. Rounded tummies, cheeks, and arms meant that you were wealthy and healthy.

Plump women were considered more attractive than skinny ones. Artists painted and sculpted images of full-figured females. Some medical doctors even encouraged people to gain weight, believing that thin women were at an increased risk of developing "nervous problems."

Diet Mania Strikes

After 1900 a thin body quickly became the American ideal, especially for females. Many factors were driving this new trend. Women's colleges were established, offering graduates an array of new career choices such as social work, journalism, law, and medicine. The idea of a "professional" appearance—one that was more like a man's—began to shape women's self-images. Exercise and athletics began taking hold of the American imagination too. Both women and men began to enjoy bicycling, golfing, swimming, yachting, rowing, horseback riding, tennis, and calisthenics.

To match their more active lifestyle, women tossed aside old dress standards—such as painful whalebone or steel corsets, stiff underclothing, and elaborate hoop dresses. They wore simpler, less restrictive clothing such as skirts and blouses. These garments could be bought, ready-made, in stores and by mail order. Such ready-made clothing introduced women to the idea of standard sizes.

Women's magazines began to regularly run

articles and ads that asked readers, "Don't you want to be thin?" In a quest to become thin, some people, especially women, sought out various diet products. They started to spend more time and energy on shrinking their bodies. Magazines and newspapers printed a variety of weight-reducing diets, including the apple and barley diet, tea and toast diet, rice and date diet, and the grapefruit diet.

Fasting also become fashionable as a quick way to drop weight. Other popular weight-loss methods of the time were electrotherapy, ingesting mineral salts, wearing rubber garments, and taking pills and laxatives. Some thought that drinking sour milk was a surefire way to lose weight. Others believed that three hot baths a day would melt off fat.

Thin Becomes In

During the 1920s, when the first large wave of diet mania had rolled across America, many people tried various weight-loss capsules and pills. Many also became sick, because capsules sometimes contained tapeworm eggs. Another early synthetic, or man-made, prescription weight-loss pill contained the substance dinitrophenol. Dinitrophenol started gaining popularity in 1918, just after the end of World War I. Newspapers and magazines hyped the drug's safety in use for weight loss. Seventeen years later, more than 100,000 Americans had tried dinitrophenol.

Then the hype turned to dismay. Newspapers and magazines began to run articles about people who became temporarily blinded from using dinitrophenol. Some people even died. By 1938 the drug had disappeared from drugstores. Today dinitrophenol is still used, but only as a powerful poisonous ingredient in some insecticides (insect killers) and herbicides (weed killers).

The year 1928 marks the first time that doctors started to prescribe extremely low-calorie diets for very overweight people. One popular diet was the Hollywood Eighteen-Day Diet. The dieter could only eat 585 calories or less each day and was restricted to grapefruits, oranges, melba toast, green vegetables, and hard-boiled eggs. The diet was promoted by citrus growers. The American Medical Association (AMA) approved a banana-and-skim-milk diet, developed by a Johns Hopkins University medical doctor.

These crash diets proved disastrous for some because they lost weight too fast. Also, many people were never meant to be thin. Several Hollywood stars actually died from these diets in the 1930s. Doctors published increasing numbers of medical reports about eating disorders and diet problems, including vomiting, as a method for weight loss.

The Frenzy Escalates

In 1956 a medical doctor wrote a diet book called *The Revolutionary Rockefeller Diet*. This was the first time a physician had authored a diet book. His low-protein, high-fat diet plan soon became trendy.

Just three years later, ninety-two diet books were in print. By the 1960s, interest in weight loss had soared even higher. The weight-loss business fed America's diet mania by publishing more fad diets and selling more weight-reduction gimmicks.

The weight-loss trend continued to grow with the introduction of low-calorie foods and soft drinks. In the meantime, the media promoted the idea that regardless of age or genetics, any female could make her body slender through dieting. Fashion photographers insisted that female models be extremely thin so that their bodies would not "compete" with the clothing.

In the mid-1960s, Twiggy, a British seventeen-year-old, arrived on the American fashion scene. Standing five feet, six inches tall and weighing only ninety-seven pounds, Twiggy became an instant icon. Many teens and young women tried to slim down in an attempt to look like Twiggy. Doctors also began to see more teens on extreme diets and with eating disorders.

Just before Twiggy arrived in the fashion world, group dieting through commercial weight-loss programs began. Weight Watchers was the first commercial weight-loss program. It was launched in 1963 by Jean Nidetch, a housewife in New York City.

Two years before, Nidetch was shopping at a local supermarket. A woman came up to her and asked Nidetch when her baby was due. Nidetch wasn't pregnant, but she was very overweight. Embarrassed, she went to the city's obesity clinic at the Department of Health. She took home their diet sheet and, by following it, began losing weight. To make dieting more fun, she started holding meetings with local housewives like herself.

At these meetings, women talked about their weight, and about the problems in their lives. Nidetch, sensing a way to make money, started charging for the meetings. Within one year, Weight Watchers made $160,000. Six years later, it had brought in $8 million. Today Weight Watchers is a huge multinational company and the world's largest weight-loss program. Since its start, 25 million people around the world have joined. Many have joined over and over again.

More Ways to Lose

Based on the success of Nidetch's Weight Watchers program, other weight-loss companies opened during the late 1960s and early 1970s. By the 1970s, those wanting to lose weight could also choose from several hundred diet books. High-protein or very low-calorie diets had many followers, as did endless grapefruit diets. Many diet books were endorsed or written by physicians. Fasting regained some popularity in the 1970s, and a flood of various diet pills hit the market.

During the 1960s and 1970s, some doctors prescribed amphetamines to weight-conscious people. Amphetamines are stimulants. These drugs "pep up" the nervous system. Unfortunately, they proved dangerous to many dieters who took them. Amphetamines increase heart rate and blood pressure and can cause anxiety, insomnia, nervousness, and addiction. With regular use, some people develop heart damage, stroke, and kidney failure. The FDA put amphetamine diet pills on its list of dangerous drugs in 1979. Doctors stopped prescribing them. Today selling, making, distributing, or using amphetamines without a prescription is illegal.

Exercising as a way to lose weight, especially for women, became more fashionable during the

1970s. Aerobic dance gained in popularity in the 1980s. A decade later, another form of aerobics emerged—step aerobics. The inventor, Gin Miller, was an Atlanta fitness instructor. While her injured knee was healing, Miller decided to keep in shape by stepping up and down on her back-porch steps.

Some dieters turned to psychology for help. They tried behavior modification therapy to help them gain control over their eating behavior. By using behavior modification techniques such as eating slowly, chewing thoroughly, and keeping a food diary, people tried to understand the factors that led to their overeating or eating of the "wrong" foods. Afterward, they hoped to be able to retrain themselves to adopt healthy eating behaviors.

Unfortunately, such techniques encourage excessive attention to eating habits, body weight, and self-control, and can lead to serious problem behaviors for people with eating disorders. Thus, behavior modification sometimes led people to develop eating disorders.

The media began to pay attention to what medical doctors had been observing for decades—eating disorders were steadily increasing in the United States. In 1974 *Mademoiselle*, a young women's magazine widely read by teens, ran an article on eating disorders among young women and teens. A few months later, *Seventeen* followed suit. The following year, six other women's magazines published articles on eating disorders.

Where Are We Today?

"My butt is way fat," Sharlene said, looking at her backside in the mirror.

Her friend Kendra just rolled her eyes. "Are you crazy? I'm the one with the fat butt! Just look at this big ol' buffalo butt!"

"Moo . . . " Sharlene snickered.

"Moo yourself," Kendra snapped.

"You know what? We should skip the cookies and milk at snack time today."

"I have an orange . . . "

"An orange is okay, I guess. But let's split it."

Can you guess how old these two girls might be? Kids as young as four, five, and six are worried about becoming fat. Some will only eat fat-free snacks and treats, while others count calories. Many teens, especially females, believe they are overweight or fat. The truth is, most are not.

Another truth is that all of us are different. We come in all sizes, shapes, and heights. Take two friends, Susan and Roberta, for example. Both girls are sixteen years old. Susan is five feet, eight inches and weighs 146 pounds. Her friend Roberta weighs exactly the same, but is four inches shorter. Both teens play tennis, swim, bike, and plan to be college roommates after they graduate high school. Compared to a supermodel, neither teen is thin. Yet both are happy and involved with school, activities, friends, dating, and family. And neither girl sees anything wrong with herself or her weight.

Actually, no "ideal weight" exists for any person. Most teens and women cannot fit into a size eight or smaller bikini no matter how much exercising or dieting they endure. In fact, well over half of American women wear a size fourteen or larger. Current medical research shows that a person's weight is based on many factors: genes, body chemicals, metabolism, food consumed, exercise, and so on.

Yet many dieters continue to pin their hopes on quick-fix pills that promise to burn, block, flush, or otherwise eliminate fat from the body. Others turn to pills that claim to control the appetite. These hopes led to another surge of diet pill popularity during the 1990s. At that time, several new prescription diet pills like fenfluramine, phentermine, and Redux promised easy and quick weight loss. But within a few years, it was found that these "magic" diet pills had the potential to cause serious side effects.

THE BOTTOM LINE: AN EVER-GROWING INDUSTRY

Since the 1920s, when medical literature began to report more cases of anorexia nervosa, the number of people with eating disorders has steadily increased. And while not everyone develops an eating disorder, millions are caught up in the quest to lose weight. This quest has developed into America's huge weight-loss industry.

3 Commercial Weight-Loss Programs

Kelly remembers a conversation she had with her mom when she was sixteen.

"I had just started to go to this high-tech center for weight loss, and it was like, computers and blinking lights everywhere! In fact, that was what attracted me. I felt like if it was completely modern—electronic, wired, and digitized—then they must be on the cutting edge of the weight-loss business. After my very first day there, I ran home and showed my mom the computer printout of exactly how much weight I needed to lose and what I had to do in order to lose it. Ten pounds, it said; and I could take it off in just two weeks! My mom was floored! I remember her grabbing the paper out of my hand, reading it, and getting so mad. She told me, 'You don't have to lose any weight, much less ten pounds—you look just fine!' I tried to take the printout back from her, but she threw it in the garbage. 'Listen,' she

told me, 'this is ridiculous. You're five feet, two inches tall, and you weigh 109 pounds. The normal weight range for your height is 104 to 114 pounds. You do the math! You're at a healthy weight! What a rip-off! I can't believe the company even signed you up!'"

Every year, over eight million Americans pay to join a commercial weight-loss program. They have plenty of programs from which to choose: Weight Watchers, Jenny Craig, Optifast, Medifast, Health Management Resources (HMR), Physicians Weight Loss Centers, Diet Center, United Weight Control Corporation, Nutri/System, Herbalife, Dick Gregory's Bahamian Diet, Slim Time, and Weight Loss Center.

New programs are introduced regularly. At last count, there were over 10,000 weight-loss centers in the United States. These centers charge a wide range of prices, and each one offers a variety of approaches to weight loss. Each one also claims to have the exclusive answer to weight loss.

Commercial weight-loss programs vary widely in their reliability. Some offer nutritional counseling, while others reflect the latest diet fads and offer phony diet aids. Some facilities are staffed by qualified professionals, while others use inadequately trained people. Some weight-loss centers even try to sell their services to people who are at a normal weight or even underweight. Few have run long-term studies to find out how effective their programs really are.

HOW THEY'RE ALIKE

Most weight-loss centers have fairly simple plans. For example, Weight Watchers once insisted that members follow a strict portion-control exchange system. Its current program, called 1-2-3 Success, assigns members a daily point allowance. Jenny Craig usually requires members to buy the program's prepackaged foods.

In addition to diet plans and special foods, some programs also offer weight-loss medications. Until 1997 the three most common prescription medications were fenfluramine, phentermine, and Redux. Fenfluramine and phentermine were often combined into a drug called fen-phen. However, when fen-phen and Redux were found to cause heart-valve damage, the Food and Drug Administration (FDA) required that the drug labels warn users of this serious risk. Although many programs stopped prescribing these drugs to clients, several programs, including Diet Center, Optifast, Health Management Resources, and Nutri/System, continued to prescribe phentermine.

Nutri/System also recommends "herbal fen-phen," a natural alternative to the other medication. However, this product can also cause serious health problems. Its main ingredient is ephedra, an herbal also known as ma huang. A powerful stimulant, ephedra speeds up the body's system and can lead to high blood pressure, heart attacks, and even death.

Some commercial programs include exercise and behavior modification as part of their weight control plan. This makes sense, since research shows that people are more successful in losing weight when they exercise regularly and follow healthy habits.

COSTS

Stina, eighteen, decided to try a weight-loss center close to home. She attended the center's initial consultation with a diet-center professional. She said, "According to the center's computer, I was supposed to lose thirteen pounds. Since both the ad and the professional said that the first ten pounds are free, I figured it wouldn't cost much to lose all of my pounds."

Stina thrust her hands into her jean pockets. "Well, the first eight pounds came off in three weeks. That cost me $350 in food. Then I had to buy another program for the remaining five pounds. I managed to lose only three pounds more in four weeks. But I shelled out another $350 in food for that time, plus a program fee of $89. All told, I spent $789 to lose eleven pounds. Pretty expensive for a supposedly free weight-loss program."

Few insurance plans and almost no managed-care plans pay for weight-loss programs and drugs. This means that most participants pay for all costs themselves. All the centers charge an enrollment fee, which ranges from $30 to $149 for three months. In addition to this expense are the ongoing fees. For example, some programs require participants to come to the center each week for weigh-ins and coaching from a counselor. This can cost from $10 to $50 dollars a week.

Additionally, Jenny Craig, Nutri/System, Optifast, and other centers require clients to buy prepackaged low-calorie foods for at least some meals. This can add an additional cost of $50 to $90 or more a week. The grand total of expenses for one year on a weight-loss program can easily reach thousands of dollars.

While weight-loss centers can sometimes help a person with short-term weight loss, the pounds will usually creep back. The National Institutes of Health report that people who are on such programs for several weeks to a few months regain two-thirds of the weight they've lost within one year. And nearly everyone regains almost all of the weight within five years.

Byron, seventeen, is six feet tall. Over the past two years, his weight has fluctuated between 158 and 190 pounds. And during those two years, Byron has signed up with one weight-loss center after another. But the results are always temporary. "I've lost and regained at least 100 pounds on those programs," Byron said. "And that's not all I've lost—I've wasted a lot of money. I'm a repeater—and these centers are just looking for guys like me. You know how they make their money? By collecting my enrollment fee each time I lose and regain weight and join or rejoin one program or another."

Actually, the main way many weight-loss companies make money is by selling their own prepackaged foods or meal supplements. The counselors at the weight-loss centers are paid low wages, but they get commissions from the sale of food, supplements, tapes, and programs. These commissions can make up as much as half of their income.

GETTING CUSTOMERS

To attract clients, weight-loss programs advertise heavily in various media outlets. The Federal Trade Commission (FTC) regulates the advertising for weight-loss programs and has set the following requirements for their advertisements:

- If a program includes a maintenance program, then its ads must contain this statement: “For many dieters, weight loss is temporary.” The ad must also give information about the average weight-loss maintenance for people on the program.
- If an ad runs for thirty seconds or less, this statement must clearly appear: “For many dieters, weight loss is temporary.” It should also state that people should check with the companies for details about their maintenance records.
- If testimonials are used in ads, then they must represent the results customers generally achieve, unless the company also clearly and prominently tells either the generally expected results or carries a statement such as “This result is not typical. You may be less successful.”

In addition, if a company wants to claim that its clients keep weight off over a long term, they must track the success of these clients for at least two years.

COMPARING POPULAR WEIGHT-LOSS PROGRAMS

There are three types of commercial weight-loss programs:

- Very low-calorie liquid meal-replacement programs such as Optifast, Medifast, and Health Management Resources
- Food-included programs like Jenny Craig, Weight Watchers, and Nutri/System
- Menu programs such as Diet Center and Physicians Weight-Loss Centers

Very Low-Calorie Liquid (VLCL) Programs

These programs start with twelve to sixteen weeks of near-fasting. Women are allowed 400 to 800 calories a day. Men are allowed up to 1,200 calories a day. The calories come from powdered drink mixes. If participants make it through this program, they then pay to go into stabilizing or maintenance programs, where they gradually reintroduce real food into daily meals. Most VLCL programs have acceptance guidelines. At Optifast, for example, participants most be at least fifty pounds over their ideal weight, or twenty pounds over and at medical risk.

VLCL programs are hard for most people to start and stick with. A large percentage will drop out. Those who go through a VLCL program may lose twenty-five to fifty pounds. But most regain the weight once they start eating real food.

Food-Included Programs

Many food-included programs claim to provide full service: food, counseling, nutritional education, and so on. Participants spend a lot of time and energy trying to stay within well-defined food limits. They may measure foods, weigh foods, count calories, eat at specific times, or follow dietary exchanges.

In general, these programs will sign up nearly anyone who wants to lose ten or more pounds, although they are supposed to screen for eating disorders, pregnancy, and various medical conditions. Some will only accept people age eighteen or older. With a doctor's approval, though, many will accept children, preteens, and teens. Some programs, like Weight Watchers, will accept kids as young as ten without a doctor's approval.

Common complaints about food-included programs are the bad-tasting foods, inconvenience, nonprofessional counseling, and high cost. Programs that sell their own brand of foods reap large profits. That's because the food has a huge markup. Another frequent complaint is that during the initial (and usually free) consultation, the goal or ideal weight set is unrealistic.

Menu Programs

The easiest program to set up is the menu program, and there are many out there. These programs provide one-on-one counseling and nutritional education. They sell no foods except for specialty items and sometimes food supplements. Instead, they provide participants with menus to buy supermarket food. Although menu programs differ, each has its own special requirements. Some restrict certain food groups. Others require daily weigh-ins.

Program costs are based on the number of pounds a participant wants to lose. Since commercial menu programs usually don't sell food, they charge high enrollment, registration, and other fees. Their total costs run about the same as VLCL and food-included programs.

WEIGHT-LOSS CAMPS

Parents sometimes send their kids to summer weight-loss camps. Usually, these camps severely restrict food and calories, but they seldom provide preteens and teens with real tools for weight management and lifestyle change. Trained health professionals may not be part of the camp staff. Also, the teen's family isn't always taught how to help support their kid's eating changes. All these problems typically lead to the same result: former campers usually regain any lost weight.

"I was embarrassed when my mom signed me up for summer weight-loss camp," said Trevor. "It made me feel like a 'fatso.' Off to the fat-farm, Trevor, I used to think to myself. In fact, it kinda scared me. But she kept insisting that I go. Man, that was not a good summer. They kept pushing us, from morning to night—'lift this, do that, go there'—until we

were completely exhausted. And the food . . . I don't even want to remember the food. We didn't get much of it, which was okay by me because it was awful tasting.

"But you know what I remember most? It was the fact that with all the changes that I was being put through, I thought about food more than ever. After lights out at night, all the guys in my cabin talked about was food. Usually we talked about what we missed the most—hamburgers, fries, shakes, pizza, macaroni and cheese, candy bars—all the stuff we couldn't have. Sometimes I even dreamed about having a secret room full of my favorite foods."

There are weight-loss camps for adults too. One is the famous Duke Diet and Fitness Center (DFC) in Durham, North Carolina. This center is a university-based diet and exercise program. Participants range in age from eighteen to eighty. Most stay at DFC for one to four or more weeks. During this time, each person is medically examined, evaluated by trained psychologists, and receives expert nutritional counseling and an individualized exercise program.

A drawback to the DFC program is its cost. In 1997, a one-week stay cost nearly $2,500; a four-week program cost about $5,600.

THE LURE OF ADVERTISING

All commercial weight-loss services are in business for one reason—to make money. They appeal to people on an emotional level. If you compare ads from various weight-loss programs, you'll see many similarities. They often show a person who has allegedly lost weight on the program, usually accompanied by photos or home movies of the person before and after the weight loss. The ads suggest that you can do the same thing. Sometimes ads show smiling kids who say how proud they are of a parent for losing weight. Celebrities sometimes endorse weight-loss programs.

All these ads play on emotions. By losing weight, the ads promise, you, too, can feel attractive, wear sexy clothing, and get admiring looks from others. The ads also sell instant gratification, or an easy way to fix something. All you have to do, they suggest, is come to our program, pay a low introductory price, and follow some rules. That's all—and within a short time, you'll be slim and attractive.

But **beware!** Health experts advise you to ignore the hype. Don't be swayed by exaggerated weight-loss results. Also, a high price is no guarantee that a particular program will work. Focus on the facts. Joining a weight-loss program is an investment of time, money, and energy.

CHOOSING A WEIGHT-LOSS PROGRAM

Before signing up for a weight-loss program, the National Institutes of Health recommend that you research various programs. Focus on those that:

- Provide a safe program: one that is low in calories, but not low in essential nutrients. The program should include recommended United States Daily Allowances (USDA) for vitamins, minerals, and protein.

- Offer a slow and steady program. Although you may lose a little more weight at first, one to two pounds per week is a reasonable long-term goal.
- Offer a maintenance program. If a weight-loss program doesn't offer a balanced program of eating and activity, you'll gain the weight back.

Before signing with any weight-loss program, talk with your doctor. This is especially important if you have health problems, take medications, or want to lose more than fifteen to twenty pounds.

You still need to do a little more research. Ask the staff at the weight-loss centers plenty of questions. Write down the answers so you can compare various programs.

GOOD WEIGHT-LOSS PROGRAMS

Some weight-loss programs can help people lose weight and maintain their loss. Good weight-loss programs:

- Are run by qualified medical and nutritional experts.
- Consider the person's age, lifestyle, and weight goals when developing a

Questions to Ask	WARNING!
Are there any health risks?	Some health risks can be extremely serious.
What statistics can you show me that prove your program works?	Don't believe testimonials, which are claims from individuals who've tried a program or diet plan. Testimonials have no scientific merit.
Is there a weight-loss maintenance plan?	More people stick to a diet program when regularly supervised.
Do people keep off the weight after they leave your program?	Ask for results over a two-to-five-year period. The Federal Trade Commission (FTC) requires weight-loss companies to back up their maintenance claims.
Is there a safe, personalized exercise program?	Exercise promotes weight loss and helps maintain it. Exercise burns calories, uses fat

	stores ,and builds muscle tissue. Because muscle burns more calories than fat, exercise boosts calorie-burning capacity.
How long before I will meet my goal weight?	Slow, consistent weight loss is best. Health professionals recommend losing no more than one pound per week. Some people may lose more at first.
What is the program's format?	Group settings offer peer support. One-to-one counseling focuses on individual needs.
Are all five major food groups included in the plan?	If no, the program is unhealthy. A good food plan emphasizes a high complex carbohydrate and low-fat diet. It contains a minimum of 1,200 calories.

Does the food taste good? Can I taste any of the prepackaged foods?	Some prepackaged foods taste pretty bad. See if you can sample some. Will you soon be bored with the food options?
Will the program help me make safe, positive behavior changes?	A good program teaches you how to live a healthier lifestyle.
What are the costs for membership, weekly fees, food, supplements, maintenance, and counseling? Do you give refunds if I drop out? If yes, how are refunds determined?	Get a price quote on every part of the program. Often, advertised fees don't include the cost of prepackaged foods, supplements, exercise videos, audiotapes, maintenance programs, and so on. Fees and additional costs should be clearly stated, with no hidden costs. Avoid programs that require large sums of money up front instead of pay-as-you-go. Find out the payment schedule and whether

	any costs are covered under health insurance. Get a copy of the refund policy.
How is my health status determined before I can participate in a particular program?	Some weight-loss programs require a medical check-up and a written OK from a medical doctor before people can start.
What are the staff's credentials? What professional supervision is provided?	Be sure staff has training in nutrition and behavior change techniques. See if a registered staff dietitian will help plan and evaluate your weight-loss program. Nutrition education, behavioral counseling, and exercise should all be part of the program.

weight-loss plan. Good companies don't simply give standard preset calorie levels to participants. Instead of focusing on weight loss alone, they look at weight management in relation to a person's lifestyle.

- Try to help participants work through their personal barriers to weight control, such as eating in response to stress.

THE BOTTOM LINE

Many programs make grand promises but just don't deliver. The National Institutes of Health (NIH) has examined whether or not many weight-loss programs actually work. This is somewhat hard to determine, since weight-loss centers seldom collect statistics on their clients' rates of success. According to the NIH, however, available statistics have demonstrated that most weight-loss programs do not provide a lasting solution. Some people will lose weight on a weight-loss program, but the great majority of these people will gain it all back.

What contributes to the poor track record of weight-loss programs? One problem is that participants often lose weight too fast. Dropping more than one percent of body weight a week after the first few weeks is too much.

Another serious problem is the lack of medical supervision. Consultants or counselors at weight-loss programs are usually amateurs. Although they may wear white lab coats, they seldom have professional education in nutrition, health, or exercise. Many program leaders are former clients with little or no formal training.

Many weight-loss centers fail to offer a maintenance program. They only focus on losing weight in the short term. This means that if a participant eventually regains the weight lost, the program is not at fault. The blame rests on the participant for failing to keep the weight off.

Although some weight-loss companies have developed maintenance programs, this service almost always costs extra, and it is usually expensive. Results from maintenance programs are seldom documented. Yet diet centers gain from providing maintenance programs. If dieters join a weight-loss program, then remain on a maintenance program, the weight-loss center will make more profit because dieters stay dependent on the program longer.

Anyone who tries a weight-loss center program needs to watch for signs of trouble. Participants shouldn't feel fatigued or depressed during the program. The program should lead to improved appetite control, beyond a few hunger pangs, as the body adjusts to a lower-fat diet. If any health concerns arise, be sure to see a doctor.

4 Bogus Weight-Loss Products

Jeff had been overweight for as long as he could remember. Flipping through a magazine, he stopped and stared at an ad that featured a set of startling before-and-after photos. The before photo showed an obese man with an unhappy look on his face, sitting alone. In the after photo, several attractive women were feeling the same man's muscular arms. He looked slim, confident, and strong.

Jeff read the ad, which featured a new protein superdrink to help people lose weight and add muscle. "MegaLean is the meal-replacement drink that's full of vitamins, minerals, and amino acids—the building blocks of protein. Add more muscle while flushing away fat—with MegaLean. It's as easy as that!"

The ad claimed that MegaLean's unique ingredients—and how they blast away fat—were trade secrets. Hoping he had finally found an easy way to lose weight, Jeff ordered a three-month supply.

THE ONLY REAL WINNERS

Because many people are desperate to take weight off fast, they're willing to suspend their common sense and hand over money for various quack products. Some pin their hopes on pills or powdered mixes that promise to burn, block, flush or somehow eliminate fat from the body. Others turn to phony weight-loss devices, such as reducing creams or appetite-suppressing earrings.

Diet gimmicks are deceptive. They appear easy to use and promise quick results. However, most don't work and can be expensive. Some are actually unsafe. These weight-loss gimmicks do work for someone, though—they make lots of money for the manufacturers.

The number of weight-loss gimmicks and phony diet aids continues to grow. Ads for these products regularly run in magazines, books, newspapers, videos, and on the Internet, television, and radio. Health food stores, drugstores, and grocery stores sell products that promise weight loss in a few painless steps. Mail order is another popular way to advertise and sell fake diet aids.

PHONY METHODS AND DEVICES

Phony weight-loss devices range from those that don't work to those that are dangerous. At a minimum, they waste money. Here are some of the most popular fake gadgets marketed to hopeful people.

Fat-Melting Creams

Anita hated her "thunder thighs," as she called them. That's why an Internet ad caught her attention. "Slimming Contours" promised to make thighs thinner. "Problem thigh area?" read the ad. "Lose two to four inches a week. Available right now at your favorite drug or cosmetics store."

Anita literally ran to a nearby drugstore right after school. She scanned the shelves until she found it—Slimming Contours. She grabbed the small jar. Then she gasped at the price. She even asked the salesperson at the counter if the cream had been mismarked. But he assured her that it was the hottest item the store sold. "We can hardly keep Slimming Contours on the shelves," he told Anita. "Everybody wants it. And if you're concerned about the price, don't be—it has a 100 percent guarantee."

That evening, Anita rubbed the slimy, light-green cream on her thighs. Then she climbed into bed. She wondered how many inches she'd lose by morning.

No proof whatsoever exists that anti-cellulite or thigh creams work. Yet thigh creams continue to be big sellers. People want to believe that rubbing some lotion or cream on their thighs or buttocks once or twice a day will make fat disappear. It sounds easy.

Advertising hype says that thigh cream ingredients like caffeine, alpha hydroxy acids and collagen cause fat to disappear. For instance, the product labels suggest that caffeine will speed up the body's metabolism, therefore enabling the burning of fat. But there is no proof that any ingredient rubbed into the skin will cause weight loss.

In 1993 a new thigh cream ingredient called aminophylline hit the news. Aminophylline is a drug used by people with asthma to help them breathe more easily. After running some small studies, two obesity researchers claimed that their aminophylline-based cream caused women to lose extremely small amounts of fat from their thighs. Newspapers and television hyped the story. By early 1994, several thigh creams had hit the market.

However, the two researchers failed to disclose the fact that they had made deals to sell thigh cream prior to announcing their findings. They also hadn't explained to the press that their study findings were based on a very small number of participants, or that they had used questionable methods to measure reported fat loss.

Thanks to slick advertising and media frenzy, sales of thigh creams boomed. The two researchers sold their idea for thigh cream several times. They also made their own version of the cream, which was sold by the Nutri/System weight-loss program. In fact, one of the researchers was on Nutri/System's scientific advisory board.

Yet when other researchers ran their own similar studies, they found that aminophylline had no effect whatsoever on fat reduction. And even though the product doesn't work, sales of thigh creams still continue. That's partially because the FDA considers thigh creams to be cosmetics. Under current federal law, when products are sold as cosmetics, manufacturers don't need to prove that their products actually work.

"Thin Pens"

They look like regular pens, but the pen's felt tip holds a fragrance, not ink. The idea behind thin pens is that by sniffing the specially selected fragrances, users can trick the brain into thinking they have already eaten. A set of three pens—in peppermint, green apple, and banana scents—costs more than thirty dollars. If you think that a particular fragrance can actually ward off the munchies, why not light a peppermint candle? Better yet, just eat an actual banana. That's a lot cheaper *and* healthier than any diet gimmick.

Massages and Wraps

The idea behind wraps is that they draw extra water from body tissues so that you lose water weight fast. Others are meant to act like a massage, or an inflatable wrap that supposedly breaks up and reduces fat. But the truth is that wraps don't cause permanent weight loss, and massage doesn't change or eliminate fatty tissue.

A popular form of wrap is the seaweed wrap. But besides being an ineffective weight-loss method, seaweed wraps are messy. You're covered with a green, sticky seaweed paste. Then you lie down on black plastic and get wrapped up, with your arms pinned to your side. Blankets and towels are pulled on top, so you're wrapped and covered from chin to toe. Forty-five minutes later, you're unwrapped.

After scrubbing off the seaweed in a shower, the scale may show up to a pound of weight lost. This lost weight is all water, and will soon return.

Hypnosis

Francine read the ad in her local newspaper: "Lose weight with hypnosis. No more hunger, no more dieting!" For forty-five dollars, she could attend a seminar and permanently lose all the weight she wanted. At the next advertised hypnosis date, Francine went to the hotel, paid her fee, and walked into the large meeting room. About one hundred people were already in the room. Most were female.

"Hypnosis," explained the presenter, "works on your subconscious. This seminar will help you tap in to your subconscious and change its contents. You'll learn everything you need today so you can lose and maintain your weight loss forever."

The lights dimmed. "Relax," murmured the hypnotist. "Relax your body from your head to your toes. Relax your forehead, relax your eyes, relax your nose, relax your chin, relax your neck, relax your shoulders . . . " After the participants had supposedly reached a state of deep relaxation, the hypnotist asked everyone to silently repeat several messages: "'I am a thin person.' 'I eat healthy food.' 'I exercise every other day.'"

That evening, Francine enjoyed her dinner of steamed fish and vegetables. During the next few days, she continued to eat low-fat meals. But by the fifth day, she could no longer fight off a chocolate craving. Subliminal messages could not keep her from scarfing two chocolate bars.

Francine felt absolutely terrible, but she decided to give hypnosis another try. This time, she went to a five-week community education class. The class, which cost eighteen dollars a week, was held at a local high school. Instead of plush seats, the ten participants sat at school desks. To reach a relaxed state, everyone lay down on the scratchy carpeting. The hypnotist led the class through another routine of relaxation and visualizations. The outcome: not a single participant in the class had lost weight over the five-week period. Several had even gained more weight!

At the last session, the class confronted the hypnotist with their poor results. The hypnotist just shrugged. "Obviously," he said, "your subconscious is in the process of fighting with your unhealthy habits."

Francine never lost weight through hypnosis; few people do. Hypnosis promises a safe and easy way to lose weight. Yet hypnosis sessions are often taught by people with questionable credentials. Most hypnotists are not trained as psychologists.

Sweating It Off

There are lots of sweating-off-the-pounds gimmicks around, such as saunas, rubber or plastic suits, or getting pelted with high-pressure water from hoses. These methods are sometimes used by athletes or people in performance arts, such as gymnasts, wrestlers, martial artists, boxers, bodybuilders, figure skaters, dancers, and distance runners.

Any weight loss that results from taking saunas or wearing rubber suits is from fluid loss and is temporary. The fluid is regained when the person eats or drinks. If teens become dehydrated by losing too much body water, they can suffer a loss of endurance and muscle performance. Also, rapid and excessive fluid loss can cause a chemical imbalance in the body, leading to heart-rhythm irregularities.

More Diet Gimmicks

Have you seen ads for some of these other phony diet devices?

Electrical muscle stimulators have a legitimate use in physical therapy treatment. But the FDA took some off the market when it was found that they were being promoted for use in weight loss and muscle toning. Not only do they not work for this, but if they are used incorrectly, muscle stimulators can be dangerous. Some users have been burned or have gotten electrical shocks from using muscle stimulators.

Appetite-suppressing eyeglasses are a complete hoax. These are common eyeglasses with colored lenses. The ads claim that the glasses can project an image onto the retina which will supress the desire to eat. There is no evidence that these eyeglasses work to curb the appetite.

Diet patches have been widely advertised. The ads claim that the patches contain a substance that is absorbed into the skin, entering the bloodstream and traveling to the brain, where it "tells" the brain to ignore hunger signals. Another ad claims that a patch contains a substance that can control the body's metabolism. Despite the ads' claims that patches have been medically proven to work, all diet patches are phony.

Magic weight-loss earrings, and similar devices for the wrist or soles of the feet, supposedly stimulate acupressure points to control hunger. The manufacturers claim that if attached just before meals, the device will exert pressure on a nerve that tells the brain that the stomach is full. None of these products actually work.

Other ineffective weight-loss gimmicks include vacuum pants, battery-operated belts, diet soap, and various drinks that "detoxify" the body.

WEIGHT-LOSS DRUGS AND SUPPLEMENTS

Diet Pills

Weight-loss pills—both prescription and nonprescription—sell well. Some doctors will prescribe diet pills, and some weight-loss programs make them available to clients. According to the *Healthy Weight Journal,* one-third of teens have tried nonprescription diet pills. Nonprescription, or over-the-counter (OTC), diet pills are widely available at supermarkets and convenience stores.

Prescription Diet Pills

"They were my answer," Joanne, now twenty-one, said. "They were beauty, self-confidence, and control all wrapped up in a little pill." Her eyes still had a glint when she talked about them. "Back when I was seventeen or so, when

> *I was using them, I could be near my favorite foods—hamburgers, fries, potato chips—and you know what? I didn't feel any desire to chow down. In fact, I sometimes forgot about eating altogether!"*

Joanne was one of many people who used dexfenfluramine, a weight-loss pill sold under the name Redux. The FDA approved the prescription sale of Redux in February 1996. The drug was designed to help obese people lose weight by decreasing the appetite.

By the mid-1990s, millions of prescriptions had been written for Redux and another obesity treatment, fen-phen. Fen-phen is a combination of two obesity drugs, fenfluramine and phentermine. Fenfluramine suppresses appetite. Phentermine speeds metabolism, which helps burn calories faster. Fen-phen surged in popularity after a 1992 study showed that when taken together, the two drugs appeared to work better than either did alone.

The drugs were recommended only for the clinically obese (those who are 20 to 30 percent above their desired weight), and in combination with sensible eating and exercise. But some doctors prescribed the drugs for people who simply wanted to shed a few unwanted pounds. Nutri/System was the country's first diet center to offer prescriptions for these diet drugs along with its prepackaged meals. Jenny Craig soon jumped on the diet-pill bandwagon. To cash in on the craze, diet-pill clinics sprang up around the country. At the height of Redux's and fen-phen's popularity, doctors wrote more than 18 million prescriptions per month for the two drugs.

However, some concerned health professionals warned that no one knew how safe these drugs were, or how well they would work long-term. Their concerns proved correct. When people stopped taking Redux or fen-phen, the weight returned. More dangerous problems soon surfaced. Doctors began to report that the drugs increased the risk of brain damage and the development of a rare lung disease.

By September 1997, the FDA had received 144 reports of severe heart-valve damage associated with the use of these prescription diet pills. Twenty-seven patients needed heart-valve replacement surgery, and three died following the surgery. The FDA acted quickly, and on September 15, 1997, the manufacturers of Redux and fen-phen were ordered to stop selling their pills.

OTC Diet Pills

"Lose Weight Fast!
Safe, Effective Weight Loss!
FDA-Approved Diet Pills!"

Ads like this tout the surefire weight-loss results (and the supposed safety) of nonprescription diet pills. No matter what they're called—Dexatrim, Accutrim, Control, Dex-A-Diet, Diadex, Thinz, Appedrine, Prolamine, or other brand names—all these OTC diet pills contain phenylpropanolamine, commonly known as PPA. PPA is the only OTC weight-loss diet pill ingredient approved for sale by the FDA.

Since their introduction in 1979, PPA diet pills have remained big sellers in the United States. Part of the reason for their success is that they're easy to find at any supermarket, drug chain, or convenience store. Anyone can buy them. And the companies that make these diet pills spend millions of dollars each year on advertising.

PPA has been around for decades, and health professionals have run a number of studies on the drug. They continually report that PPA can cause serious problems. In fact, PPA can cause side effects similar to those caused by amphetamines, as well as other dangerous reactions like seizures and kidney failure.

What's more, studies show that PPA has little or no effect on long-term weight reduction. Pills containing PPA may keep a person from feeling hungry for a few weeks, but these diet pills don't keep weight off for long. According to Laura Fraser, contributing editor at *Health* magazine, 96 percent of the developed nations in the world have banned PPA as a diet aid because of its high risks and general ineffectiveness.

The FDA actively investigates PPA. In 1990 a congressional subcommittee heard from doctors and health professionals who testified that PPA caused many serious health problems and even death. Some doctors report that PPA increases the risk of stroke. Four years after the congressional hearings, the FDA began working with the Nonprescription Drug Manufacturers' Association (NDMA) to develop a study on PPA and its relationship to the risk of stroke. The NDMA is an organization whose members are drug manufacturers, including those companies that make PPA.

Other OTC Diet Pills

Jess popped three white tablets into her mouth, then sipped her diet soda.

"Is that lunch, Jess?" Meg asked as she unwrapped her sandwich.

Jess laughed. "No, it's better than lunch. ***You*** *eat lunch. Let everyone else eat lunch! I'm not hungry."*

Meg studied her friend's face. "What exactly ***is*** *that you're taking?"*

Jess slid the bottle toward her friend. "It's really cool! It's a new, scientific way to speed up your metabolism! I just take two tablets a day. They make my body burn fat faster, so I lose weight without exercising. And I don't feel hungry between meals."

"Like a gym in a pill!" Meg exclaimed, taking a bite of her sandwich. "What'll they think of next?" She paused. "So . . . what's in them that makes them so good?"

"Organic herbs and algae."

"Yuck!"

"They correct the imbalance in your fat cells."

"Your fat cells! What's up with that?" Meg shook her head in disbelief. "You look just fine to me . . . you know, I think the only thing imbalanced here are your taste buds!"

The FDA has banned many nonprescription ingredients that once claimed to melt fat away. In 1991,

PPA: Side Effects

- Anxiety
- Insomnia and other sleep disturbances
- Nervousness
- Headaches
- Nausea
- Jitters
- Fatigue, drowsiness
- Mood swings
- Irritability

PPA: Dangerous Reactions

- Extremely high blood pressure
- Irregular heartbeat
- Heart muscle and kidney damage
- Seizures
- Hallucinations
- Vomiting
- Disorientation
- Death from kidney failure or stroke

after a twenty-year study, the agency called 111 ingredients used in OTC diet pills either ineffective or unsafe (or both). The agency then stopped OTC pill makers from claiming on their product labels that any of these 111 ingredients actually promoted weight loss.

The Federal Trade Commission has also gone after the makers of ineffective OTC weight-loss pills. With the aid of a number of state Attorneys General, the FTC has won many cases against marketers of pills that claim to absorb, burn, or flush away fat.

Diuretics and Laxatives

Char loved competing in gymnastics. The one thing she didn't like, though, was the constant focus on weight. "Every day we had to weigh in. It was really tense right before a meet. We had to make the weight requirements—and the coach didn't care how we did it. So we'd usually pass around Ex-Lax the night before the meet."

Like Char, some teens try to lose weight by taking laxatives or diuretics. Laxatives are drugs that cause bowel movements. Water pills, or diuretics, cause the body to urinate. Although either drug can effect some weight loss through dehydration, the water weight is quickly replaced when the products are no longer used. Neither laxatives nor diuretics reduce body fat. Instead, the flushing effect of these drugs causes a loss of important vitamins and minerals. This keeps important nutrients like calcium from being properly absorbed. Calcium is essential for healthy bone growth. Abuse of these pills can also lead to irregular heart functioning and kidney damage.

Tolerance can quickly develop with ongoing use of laxatives. Instead of taking one or two tablets, abusers must take more and more in order to produce the original effects, sometimes taking up to sixty or more tablets a day. Laxative abuse can cause diarrhea, fatigue, nausea, stomach cramps, bloating, and pain. Regular abuse of laxatives can eventually cause the loss of electrolytes, which regulate the heart's functions. As electrolyte levels drop, the risk of irregular heartbeats—and even of heart attacks—increases. Ongoing use of laxatives can also cause severe damage to the colon, eventually causing an inability to function properly. Once this state is reached, the colon must be surgically removed.

Dietary Supplements As Weight-Loss Aids

Lacy slowly sipped from her steaming mug of herbal tea.

"Dieter's tea!" Darlene exclaimed, lighting a cigarette and looking at the box of tea bags on the table. "That's funny. Remember the 'smoker's tea' I was drinking by the gallon?"

"That was different," Lacy said. "Smoking is an addiction. You can't beat it with just ***tea.****"*

Darlene exhaled a plume of smoke. "Maybe. Anyway, not only did the tea not work for me, but I think it actually made me sick."

Lacy took another sip. "You were sick from nicotine withdrawal! You had that monkey on your back! But seriously . . . how could this stuff be bad for you? It's all natural—I got it at the health food store."

Lacy might be surprised at some of the ingredients in her dieter's tea. Some herbs act as laxatives or diuretics. They can also cause cramps, nausea, diarrhea, and a pounding heart. Long-term use of some ingredients found in so-called dieter's teas can lead to colon and heart damage or even death.

Dietary supplements come in many forms, such as tablets, capsules and liquids. They might include vitamins, minerals, fibers, herbs, and other botanicals, amino acids, concentrates, and extracts.

Fad Diets

Fad diets, like the cabbage soup diet, have long been popular. Various ones go in and out of fashion. Basically, fad diets tend to emphasize one food or food group and eliminate others—in other words, they advocate unbalanced diets. There are many, many fad diets, but most fall into five categories: "magical" foods, high-protein/low-carbohydrate, high-fat, liquid diets or meal-replacement shakes, and fasting.

"Magical" Food Diets

During the 1990s, the cabbage soup diet was just one of many so-called magical food diet fads. While several versions of the diet circulated around the United States, each included the all-you-can-eat, "fat-burning" cabbage soup. The soup's main ingredients were typically cabbage, carrots, celery, tomatoes, peppers, and onions. After a week on the diet, people could supposedly lose up to seventeen pounds.

Nonprescription Substances the FDA Says Are *Not* Diet Aids

- Alcohol
- Alfalfa
- Anise Oil
- Arginine
- Caffeine
- Dextrose
- Guar gum
- Wheat germ
- Yeast
- Xanthum gum

However, any weight loss that large and that quick will be mostly due to water loss, particularly from diarrhea. Body fat will not be lost. And any weight lost will come back fast once a person returns to regular eating habits.

Many fad diets also use pseudoscience. The cabbage soup diet, for example, claims that "your body will utilize the soup's potassium, carbohydrates, protein, and calcium to lessen your craving for sweets." The diet promises to cleanse the body of "impurities"—a classic claim of fad diets—but only if the diet is followed exactly. But fad food diets are terribly monotonous. Most people get bored with such a restrictive set of food no-no's and usually break the diet quickly. That's how the promoters of the diet get away with less-than-promised results.

Looking to escape for a few minutes from the boring research project they had been assigned at school, Darcy and Gino entered a new Internet search word on Gino's computer. An entire list of diets—both their names and full instructions—quickly came up on the screen. Gino was immediately drawn to one underlined in blue because he recognized the name. He clicked onto the link and was taken to the diet's Web page.

"Take a look at this diet, Darcy," he said.

"The New Mayo Clinic Diet! I didn't know they had a Web page for that!"

Gino smiled. "I know. The Mayo Clinic is pretty famous."

Gino printed the home page from the New Mayo Clinic Diet. The diet was several pages long, with an explanation of how and why the particular combination of foods it advocated maximized the body's potential for burning fat. Darcy looked over the pages.

"Wow," she said. "Can this be right? I mean, how could any decent diet tell you to eat all the eggs and butter you want? And look," she said, flipping through the pages, "there's grapefruit included for like every meal."

"That does seem kinda odd, I guess," Gino replied. "But you know," he continued, looking at the allowable foods and their portions, "it sure looks like it ***tastes*** *better than anything else I've seen."*

"Yeah, but all that fat and cholesterol? I

Dietary Supplement	Description
Bee pollen	Bee pollen contains starch, sugars, protein, and a little fat. It can cause an allergic reaction in some people.
Bulk producers or fillers	Some fiber-based products may absorb liquid or swell in the stomach, and may temporarily reduce hunger. But some fillers can cause blockage in the intestines, stomach, or esophagus. The FDA has taken legal action against the makers of some of these products.
Carnitine	Carnitine is a body chemical made up of lysine and methionine, two essential amino acids. No proof exists that it provides energy or reduces body fat.
Chromium picolinate	Found in supplements, shakes, and nutrition bars. According to *Health* magazine, nine million Americans

	took chromium supplements in 1995. Chromium is naturally and abundantly found in many foods: broccoli, black pepper, mushrooms, potatoes, peanut butter, and whole grains. Chromium deficiency is rare. Only a tiny amount of chromium is needed for proper metabolism. Any extra chromium in the body is eliminated through urination. No proof exists that extra chromium increases muscle mass, burns fat, or raises metabolism.
Ephedrine or ma huang	Ma huang, a Chinese herb, contains a stimulant called ephedrine. No proof exists that ephedrine helps people lose weight. Yet many herbal diet teas and remedies contain ephedrine or ma huang.

Ephedrine or ma huang (continued)	If used improperly or taken for too long, ephedrine can cause high blood pressure, rapid heartbeat, muscle injury, and nerve damage.
Ergogenic aids	Ergogenic means possessing the potential to increase work output. Phony ergogenic aids promise to pump up muscles and speed metabolism and therefore increase weight loss. Ads read: "Blast your body with energy!" or "Guaranteed new muscle growth." Hundreds of ergogenic aids are sold, including amino acids such as arginine and ornithine, brewer's yeast, choline, co-enzymes or enzymes, creatine, inositol, lecithin, kelp, PABA, pangamic acid, wheat

	germ, wheat germ oil, and various herbs. No scientific evidence exists to prove that they work.
Fat and starch blockers	Fat or starch blockers promise to absorb or block the digestion of starches and fats, but they simply don't work. They can cause nausea, vomiting, diarrhea, and stomach pains.
Glucomannan	Glucomannan is a plant root advertised as the "weight-loss secret of the Orient for over 500 years." No evidence exists to support this claim.
Herbal diet teas	Many "diet" teas are basically regular tea with a few herbs. Other herbal teas aren't tea at all. They are made of herbs, flowers, spices, and other parts of plants. Herbal teas haven't been shown to

Herbal diet teas (continued)	cause weight loss. Because they can cause harmful effects, avoid teas containing these herbs: comfrey, lobelia, woodruff, tonka beans, melilot, and sassafras root.
Herbal fen-phen	Herbal fen-phen is just a combination of herbals, and is NOT similar to the prescription drug combination of fenfluramine and phentermine. In early 1998, the FDA began taking action to stop the sale of herbal fen-phen products.
Spirulina	Spirulina is a species of blue-green algae that has not been proven effective for losing weight.

wouldn't do it. Maybe you could ask your doctor, or e-mail the Mayo Clinic and ask if this really is their diet."

Gino shook his head and printed another copy of the diet for himself. "I don't see what the problem is. It's the New Mayo Clinic Diet! If it says it's from the Mayo Clinic, then what's the issue? Besides," he smiled, as he thought about planning some delicious meals, "this is the first diet I've seen in a long time that I could actually live with!"

Some fad diets use a respected medical name in order to fool unsuspecting people. These diets are especially dangerous. Many people will not examine the diet critically, but instead simply accept the various claims it makes and follow its instructions. One false "Mayo Clinic" diet, for example, says to eat until stuffed, even if this includes as much meat or eggs as the person wants. Fake Mayo Clinic diets have been passed around for decades. The world-famous Mayo Clinic in Rochester, Minnesota, regularly denies any connection with or endorsement of these diets. A grapefruit version of a fake Mayo diet is more than twenty years old and is still circulating among hopeful dieters today.

High-Protein/Low-Carbohydrate Diets

These diets are based on eating few, if any, carbohydrates, such as bread, potatoes, pasta, and whole grains. Instead of these high-energy foods, dieters are instructed to eat eggs, beef, poultry, fish, cheese, and other high-protein foods. But since these foods are often high in fat and cholesterol, this diet, if followed long-term, can cause heart problems.

Low-carbohydrate diets have been around for over 100 years. During the late 1990s, *The Zone,* another low-carbohydrate diet book, remained on the *New York Times* bestseller list for twelve weeks and sold over 1 million copies. The book's author, Barry Sears, a Ph.D. in biochemistry, pushes high-fat foods such as poultry, fish, and nuts and instructs dieters to avoid carbohydrates such as bananas, brown rice, and sweet potatoes. The reason? He says that too many carbohydrates build fat.

Many experts disagree with Sears' theory and say that his diet principles are unproven. The Zone diet, and similar diets such as the Air Force Diet or the Doctor's Quick Weight Loss Diet, are rarely based on sound research. In fact, low-carbohydrate diets can lead to bad breath, headaches, fainting, dehydration, and intense cravings for carbohydrates, especially candy.

High-Fat Diets

Dr. Atkins' Diet Revolution, both the old and new versions, is an example of a high-fat diet. It eliminates most carbohydrates and instead encourages dieters to load up on fatty foods such as butter, mayonnaise, bacon, eggs, and cheese.

Yet scientific studies clearly show that when carbohydrate intake is too low, the body burns fat incompletely. Substances called ketones are then produced. Ketones can irritate the kidneys. An abundance of ketones in the bloodstream results in a condition called ketosis, which can lead to dry mouth, weakness, fatigue, dizziness, nausea, and other problems. High-fat diets can also increase the risk of obesity, heart disease, and artery damage.

Liquid Diets or Meal-Replacement Shakes

Heather recalled what she thought of as her "year of the liquid lunch."

*"It was when I was fourteen. I remember walking into my neighborhood deli, and they were right there above the milk—all those cans of Slim-Fast. It's got lots of vitamins and minerals and has only 220 calories, and it comes in lots of flavors. Well, I had just broken up with my boyfriend, and I was feeling pretty bad about everything. I was pounding down every cookie and piece of cake I could get my hands on. I couldn't stop—eating was the only thing that seemed to fill up all the empty space I felt inside of me. Anyway, I saw all these cans, like vanilla, strawberry, chocolate—**chocolate** shakes! I started drinking them for every meal."*

The Slim-Fast diet plan recommends that dieters drink their shakes to replace two meals each day. Only one meal of solid food per day is allowed. In the beginning, some people have success with liquid diets. But most get bored with the monotony and quickly return to regular foods. Once off the liquid diet, most people regain any lost weight.

Liquid diets obtained through weight-loss centers are extremely expensive. Such shakes are also sold through marketers such as Herbalife, Nu Skin, and Shaklee. Most of these programs are supposed to be supervised by doctors or other medical and health professionals. However, most teens on liquid diets aren't supervised by anyone. Instead, teens simply buy the products at supermarkets and drugstores.

Whatever the source, low-calorie liquid diets can deprive people of important nutrients and are potentially dangerous. The side effects are so serious that the FDA requires manufacturers to put a warning label on high-protein, low-carbohydrate liquid diet drinks.

When teens use these products incorrectly, they can suffer side effects such as nausea, dizziness, fatigue, hair loss, irritability, and irregular menstruation (periods). If teens use them as a sole source of nutrition for a prolonged time, serious health problems and even death can result.

Fasting

At dinner, Doug pushed his plate away. He said, "The pasta looks great, Mom, but I'm not eating today. Actually, not today or tomorrow. I've got a wrestling meet in two days, and it's the only way I'm gonna make weight."

Doug's mother was concerned. "Eat just a little, Doug. Something to hold you over. I don't like this skipping-meals thing. And I think you'd do better at the meet if you had some food inside you."

"You know how strict Coach is, Mom," Doug replied, clearing his plate and silverware from the table. "Besides, I've heard that

fasting is good for you. It cleans out the toxins from your body and gives you a clear and focused mind."

On the day of the meet, Doug had no trouble making weight. But a few seconds after he began wrestling, he felt uncomfortably light-headed and dizzy. It took him by surprise. He started to panic as he felt his strength start to slip away. It didn't take long for his opponent to easily win the match.

Fasting is when a person eats and drinks very little, or nothing at all, for a period of time. Sometimes people fast for religious purposes, but this is usually for just a few hours or half a day. Fasting for longer periods of time is not a healthy way to lose weight. For health, growth, and energy, the body needs a fresh supply of nutrients daily.

Doug's statements about the benefits of fasting are not true. Fasting is the same as starvation, because the body receives no food. Fasting doesn't rid the body of toxins. It puts a huge strain on the organs, especially the heart, kidneys, and liver. During a fast, the body fails to receive important minerals known as electrolytes. Electrolytes allow the heart to beat correctly. Fasting can lead to dangerous heart problems, even if the person has no prior history of heart trouble. Weight loss resulting from prolonged fasting can also increase the risk of gallstones.

After just a few days of fasting, the body is thrown into ketosis. This state can lead to dry mouth, weakness, fatigue, dizziness, nausea and other problems. For energy, the body begins to burn up fat, muscle, and organs. An even longer fast can lead to anemia, liver malfunction, kidney stones, and other serious problems.

WHAT ABOUT FAT-FREE FOODS?

Eating fat-free and reduced-fat foods seems to be a safe way to lose weight. Americans have plenty of these foods to choose from, such as cold cereals, yogurt, ice cream, granola bars, and lunch meats, as well as fruits and vegetables, which usually contain very little or no fat.

Fat is the current nutritional villain in America. Before fat, it was sugar, starch, and cholesterol. Today people count fat grams, checking the labels on boxes and cans. And they buy a lot of fat-free foods, especially desserts and snacks.

However, it's hard to make good-tasting desserts and snacks without using fats. Fat helps to carry flavor and texture. Fat is one of the main reasons why cookies, cakes, candy bars, and muffins taste good and are satisfying. Many fat-free desserts and snacks don't taste very good.

Although these products contain little or no fat, fat-free goodies usually have the same—or higher—number of calories as their full-fat versions. That's because extra sugar or sugary fillers are used to replace the missing fat. They may be low in fat but, like their full-fat versions, they still provide lots of calories. Because they are low in fat, people assume they won't cause weight gain and therefore gobble up extra helpings of anything labeled "diet," "low-calorie," "low-fat," or "fat-free."

THE BOTTOM LINE ON BOGUS WEIGHT-LOSS PRODUCTS

Any product or fad diet that claims people can lose weight quickly and without effort is bogus. The only way to lose weight safely is to lose it slowly by reducing the number of calories you eat and by increasing your level of exercise. Very low calorie diets and fasts can be risky and require medical supervision. Otherwise, these weight-loss methods are dangerous.

Fad diets rarely have any permanent effect on weight loss. Sudden and radical changes in eating patterns are hard to maintain over time. In addition, so-called crash or quick-weight-loss diets often send people into a cycle of weight gain once regular eating resumes. These people then find it even more difficult to reduce when they try dieting again.

5 Why Diet Plans and Programs Don't Work

Every week millions of people eagerly read what Jane Brody writes about nutrition and health. The author of several nutrition books, Brody is the personal health columnist for the *New York Times*. Her column appears in hundreds of local newspapers across the country. In the July/August 1996 issue of the *Nutrition Action Healthletter*, Brody talked about her own dieting history.

After a few extra pounds crept on, Brody turned to a few popular diets to lose weight. Sometimes she was successful, but she would inevitably regain the weight, along with some extra pounds. At one point, she weighed thirty-five pounds more than her ideal weight. Finally, she realized that *diets don't work*. They left her feeling deprived, bored, and angry—eating grapefruit, or eggs and bacon, or whatever the popular fad diet was. As she got fatter, she had even tried fasting all day and eating only one meal at night. But after starving all day, she would find herself compulsively stuffing food into her mouth.

One day Brody gave up and decided that she'd just be healthy and fat. She tossed all her diet books, gimmicks, and gadgets. She started to eat regular meals three times a day, along with some light snacks. Each day she enjoyed a favorite treat, like a couple of cookies or a slice of pie. She also started exercising regularly. Every day she would walk, cycle, or swim. Her exercise goal was to have fun, not to work out until she was exhausted.

Little by little, Brody lost weight. Twenty-five years later, she's never regained those thirty-five extra pounds.

ANTI-DIET RESEARCH

As Jane Brody and many experts have discovered, diets don't work. In 1992 even the federal government acknowledged that dieting was an ineffective way to lose weight. That year, the National Institutes of Health assembled a panel of health experts, who announced that all their patients who had lost weight through behavior-modification programs and diets of 1,200 calories or less per day, had regained the weight within five years. Most of them had put it back on within a year.

Early Research

The first large anti-diet study was run during World War II. Ancel Keys, a University of Minnesota researcher, published a two-volume report on the effects of semi-starvation on conscientious war objectors. In 1944 thirty-six young men volunteered for Keys' nine-month study. For three months, the men ate regular meals and exercised. Next, they went on a semi-starvation diet with vitamin and mineral supplements. This diet was similar to those offered by today's weight-loss programs.

The men lost weight. But they became depressed and argumentative. Fatigued and listless, they couldn't complete most of their everyday activities. Most thought about food constantly. And because they were always hungry, they had little mental energy to think about anything else.

After the period of restrictive dieting ended, the men overate continuously. Even though they were now allowed to eat as much as they wanted, they reported that they still felt hungry all the time. All the men regained weight, but much of what was formerly muscle mass was now being replaced with pounds of fat. This study clearly showed that people placed on a restrictive diet experience the same symptoms of today's regular dieters: depression, anxiety, and food preoccupation, followed by bingeing and weight gain.

In 1958 the University of Pennsylvania School of Medicine reviewed hundreds of published studies on obesity treatment, spanning thirty years of medical literature. The careful and thorough analysis showed that 90 to 95 percent of all diets fail. No comparable medical study since then has been able to show a higher long-term success rate.

By the 1970s, some researchers began to link dieting to eating disorders. Researchers at Northwestern University found that dieting usually leads to bingeing and the many problems that go along with it, such as depression and feelings of failure. They also showed that dieting causes people to lose touch with their stomach's real cues of hunger and fullness.

Current Anti-Diet Research

Diet studies continue to be undertaken today. Here are some findings from a recent study at the University of Toronto:

- Dieting disrupts people's sense of when and how much to eat, and it often leads to overeating. It teaches people to ignore the natural physical feelings of hunger and fullness that regulate weight and can often cause people to ignore other feelings, such as disappointment and anxiety. Instead, dieters use food to manage their feelings.
- People can learn to stop dieting. University of Toronto researchers developed an "undieting program," which focuses on teaching people to eat normally and accept themselves at their present body size.
- When people stop dieting, they are generally happier, have fewer eating problems, and feel better about themselves.

THE SELLING OF AMERICA

Jenny is sixteen and already a veteran of numerous phony fad and meal-replacement diets. She felt like she had been taken in by the allure of clever advertising's magical promises. But she realized something. Despite all the claims and guarantees made by these ads and products, Jenny would never achieve the physical ideal of an ultra-thin model. It just wasn't **her** *body. There* **was** *no magic to losing weight. Any weight she had ever lost through one of those diets or plans went back on within a few months.*

Jenny is now a healthy eater, as well as a more realistic person. She eats what she likes in moderation and swims three times a week at the local YWCA. Her attempts at fast weight loss have made her aware of how easily people can be influenced. She has realized how clever and powerful advertising can be.

She says, "I think that the advertising for weight-loss products and programs works exceptionally well—for the companies, that is. The ads show the unhappy before photo—and then the after photo, where the person is looking slim and happy—and it makes you think, if they can do it, why can't I? The ads prey on people's weakness and insecurity. Everyone wants to be beautiful, everyone wants to be loved. And the advertisers know it.

"I think the ads are especially persuasive during the winter months. That's when I used to put on the most weight, because I was less active, and because of the holiday season. There are always so many cookies and other goodies around from November to New Year's. I also think that magazines and talk shows send the message that I should make losing weight my number-one New Year's resolution. But you know, I've got to hand it to the

weight-loss people. They do a great job of advertising—they've actually created a mind-set. My friends and I used to go out and buy every new diet product."

Advertising Is Powerful

Although the federal government and many medical professionals have proven that diets don't work, millions of people still believe that they do. Why? One major reason is advertising. The ads for weight-loss centers and diet products are selling hope, and their appeals are purely emotional. They touch on many different and strong feelings: the dream to be popular, attractive and sexy; the fear of being laughed at or rejected by others; the desire for instant gratification. The ads promise an instantly slim body with no work, no fuss, no bother. They imply that by following a few simple instructions, anyone can easily obtain the perfect body. Once the perfect weight is reached, a person will gain self-esteem and popularity. No wonder people find it hard to ignore or even downplay such appealing messages.

The ads also assert the idea that there is a "secret" to weight loss. Once the secret is revealed, dieters will then be able to lose weight and keep it off—at least that's what promoters of diet products and programs want you to believe.

Advertising for weight-loss products and programs goes on year-round, but winter is both the main season for gaining weight and the big time of year for trying to lose it. According to a study published in the October 1995 issue of *Supermarket Business* more than half of the consumers surveyed said that they planned to go on a diet right after January 1.

Advertisements Don't Inform—They Sell

Take a close look at the advertisements for diet centers or weight-loss products. You'll find that they contain little factual information. Seldom do they reveal the specific details or the complete cost of the program or product. They rarely state information about the percentage of customers who have been successful at keeping weight off over the short or long term.

If you try to get this information from a diet center by phone, you probably won't get your questions answered. Weight-loss centers won't tell you over the telephone how many people on their programs have lost weight and kept it off long-term. Nor will they tell you about complete program costs. The diet counselor or salesperson will instead try to get you to come in for a "free" consultation. Once at the weight-loss center, you will receive a sophisticated and well-rehearsed sales pitch. At this point, many people find it hard to say "no."

DIETING MYTHS

Many people also believe—or want to believe—various myths about dieting. They diet, or try weight-loss products, because they want a quick fix. They want to believe that extra weight can be lost easily and fast. Dieters base these beliefs on nine commonly held myths.

Myth #1: All You Need Is The Right Diet

Kathy is fifteen years old; her boyfriend, Jorge, is seventeen. They met at a party during the summer. What initially attracted Kathy to Jorge was that he was a great dancer—she loved to dance. What attracted Jorge to Kathy was the way she looked. From the start, he complimented her on her body, especially her long slender arms and tiny waistline. Kathy loved the attention, and she quickly fell for Jorge. But the longer she went out with him, the more pressure she felt to keep her body exactly the way Jorge liked it.

"I guess I feel like that's the main reason he's with me," she said, picking at her nail polish. "We never really talk about anything—stuff on the news or even just what's happening in school. He's always like, 'You look beautiful today' or 'Man, I feel so proud when I walk down the street with you.' I don't know—I mean, it's nice and all, but sometimes I wonder why there isn't anything else to our relationship. He just focuses on my **looks** *all the time. And I panic every time Jorge even looks at another girl. What's worse, my insecurity has made me so nervous all the time, I've been eating a lot and I've put on some weight. I've tried at least five or six diets since September, but I just can't find one that'll work, that will just take off the pounds and keep them off. But I know it's out there. It's gotta be out there somewhere, right? All I have to do is find it. I just hope I can find it fast . . ."*

Like Kathy, many dieters believe that if they just find the right diet, they'll lose weight and keep it off, which is why she and so many others keep trying new diets. Yet scientific studies continually show the same results: Most dieters gain back any weight lost in five years or less. Only 5 to 10 percent keep the weight off permanently.

The idea that with the right plan, weight loss is easy is popularized by the media. Pick up nearly any fashion, health, or lifestyle magazine, and you'll find at least one article about weight loss, the right way to diet, and so on. The popular press continues to support the false idea that weight loss is simple once the right formula or weight-loss plan is found.

The real truth is this: If weight loss were simple, no one would need special diets or weight-loss plans, because no one would be overweight in the first place.

Myth #2: Ideal Weight Is the Dieting Target

Life insurance companies print weight charts that show the "ideal" weight for a man or woman's height and age. These weights are based on the height and weight of millions of people insured by major life-insurance companies. The companies took these numbers and determined the average weight of people at given heights. Those weights were then called *ideal.*

But there's a major problem with this method of determining ideal weight—the insurance companies didn't measure skeletal structure. Some people of similar height naturally weigh more than others. Therefore, some people who—according to these charts—are "overweight" are not in reality fat. Besides, there is no such thing as an ideal weight for anyone. Everyone's weight fluctuates during the day, from month-to-month, and over the life course.

Myth #3: Stop Dieting, and You'll Gain and Gain

Jane Brody clearly showed that by *not* dieting, she maintained a healthy weight. When you're on a diet and feeling hungry, your body adjusts its metabolism. You may crave sweets and carbohydrates or you may feel tired. Your body is telling you that it is hungry.

Studies also point out that genetics play an important part in natural weight. For example, when identical twins grow up in separate homes, they weigh almost the same throughout their lives. Also, the weight of adopted children usually reflects that of their biological parents, not their adoptive ones. This research suggests that everyone has a genetically determined weight range that the body seeks to maintain. This weight may not be the same as the ideal weight on an insurance company's chart.

Myth #4: Lose Weight, and You'll Be Healthy

It's true that being seriously overweight, or obese, can increase health risks. But being skinny doesn't guarantee a longer, healthier, or happier life. In fact, being severely underweight also increases many health risks and can even lead to death.

Myth #5: The Faster You Lose Weight, the Faster You'll Reach Your Weight Goal

In general, the opposite is true: The faster a person tries to lose weight, the faster the weight returns.

Here's why: The human body tries very hard to maintain its current weight. It does so by a highly regulated system. If a person eats more calories than usual, the body tries to burn them off. But if a person eats fewer calories than usual, the body tries to save on energy by slowing its metabolism.

Myth #6: The Quickest (and Best) Way to Lose Weight Is to Fast

Starvation is the ultimate diet. By not taking in any energy, people must live entirely on their own energy stores. So, starvation actually is the fastest way to lose weight.

But fasting is extremely dangerous. Starvation involves real hunger, and real hunger doesn't go away until a person eats. If starving people don't eat, they will eventually die.

Fasting forces the body to burn both fat and protein. The body gets the energy it would normally obtain from food from lean muscle mass or major organs. This use of essential protein can have deadly consequences. Prolonged fasting can produce permanent muscle damage, especially to the heart. Starvation causes the liver and kidneys to work harder, speeding up the body's elimination of valuable vitamins, minerals, and proteins.

"My senior prom!" Dvora wrote in her journal. "I can't believe it's finally here! I want it to be perfect. I found this mad sexy dress—shiny, short, and black. When I tried it on, though, I had this little stomach roll, and that gave me some trouble with the zipper, but never mind that! I've got ten days. I figure if I don't eat any-

thing until then, me and that dress will make a serious entrance at the prom!"

There's something Dvora should realize: the weight gain that follows starvation is mostly fat. Repeated starvation cycles seriously reduce muscle mass and increase fat mass. This makes further attempts at weight loss even harder.

Myth #7: Everyone's Dieting . . . So Dieting Must Work

It's true that many people are dieting at any given time. But if dieting worked, then why would so many people need to keep returning to a weight-loss program or try yet another diet?

Jon noticed something after he enrolled in his fourth weight-loss program. "The weight-loss centers make most of their money by collecting my enrollment fee over and over, each time I regain weight and rejoin the program. I've seen many of the same people in my classes. We're all repeaters."

Authors Diane Epstein and Kathleen Thompson asked the diet-program counselors they interviewed for their book *Feeding on Dreams* how many of their clients were "repeaters." The counselors estimated that 70 to 80 or even 90 percent of diet-program clients are repeaters. The weight-loss centers couldn't stay in business without them.

Weight-loss centers know that dieting doesn't work—they thrive on this fact. That's why most don't publicize their rates of success. And that's also why some offer reduced rates to their repeat clients.

Myth #8: If I Could Just Stay Away from "Bad" Foods . . .

Dieting sets people up for an unrealistic and unhealthy attitude toward food. People begin to think of food in terms of "good" or "bad." But food is neither good nor bad—it's just food. Yet people constantly attribute certain qualities to specific food items. If they eat something they consider bad, they feel guilty; if they don't eat what they crave, they feel deprived. Dieting sets up a vicious cycle of shame and deprivation.

Myth #9: Okay, So Diets Don't Work for Most People—Maybe *I'm* an Exception

People keep returning to weight-loss centers and keep trying new diet products, hoping that they can somehow beat the odds.

Various weight-loss programs offer lots of different services, but they don't actually differ that much in concept. For instance, all weight-loss programs offer diets. But while the diets may vary—liquid diets, low-calorie, menu diets, and so on—none of them will work long-term.

Weight-loss products also vary, from candy and gum to herbs and rubber suits. But like the programs, weight-loss products don't work to keep weight off in the long term. Few even work short-term!

Want proof? Try asking weight-loss center representatives for the percentage of their clients who are repeat dieters. They probably won't tell you this information. The weight-loss industry is heavily dependent on these repeat dieters. This dependence clearly shows that it is nearly impossible to make diet behavior part of a normal lifestyle.

Through repeated dieting, people lose touch with their natural hunger signals. Instead, they follow the instructions of a weight-loss program. They stop questioning their desire for real food—say, freshly cooked pasta with lightly sautéed vegetables sprinkled with good cheese. Instead, they eat what the weight-loss center gives to them—a tasteless, low-calorie package of mushy pasta and limp vegetables coated in a fake butter sauce.

THE BOTTOM LINE

Weight loss—whether through a weight-loss program, a diet, or the use of herbs, pills, liquids, or devices—can affect your physical and mental health. The health problems caused by regular dieting are potentially more dangerous than problems you may have, for example, with your teeth, feet or skin. Yet dentists, podiatrists, and dermatologists are trained and licensed professionals. The people who sign you up for a weight-loss program or convince you to part with $24.95 for their diet book are *salespeople.*

Weight-loss centers are a *business.* In most states, they are unregulated. And anyone can promote a diet plan, a diet book, or a weight-loss product. The author, promoter, or seller needn't be a nutritionist or trained health professional.

Getting the correct message out—that diets don't work—takes hard work and education. The number of anti-diet professionals in the United States is growing. These professionals include health educators, nutritionists, psychologists, and dietitians.Their message: Forget about diets and weight-loss programs and products.

6 Consequences

Dieting has many negative effects. Because it can injure the body and even cause death, dieting is dangerous. It can lead to serious health problems. For example, dieting can stunt or stop children's and teens' growth. It can also interfere with mental and physical development.

Diets disrupt normal, healthy eating patterns, and they can trigger eating disorders. Beyond the money and time lost on ineffective or fake weight-loss products and programs, diets sap energy and strength. And chronic dieting causes obsessive food, weight, and body-image preoccupation.

DIETING SABOTAGES THE METABOLISM

Dieting affects the body's natural metabolism. Metabolism is the rate at which the body converts food into fuel. When people diet and reduce their caloric intake, the body adjusts to that new level and uses fewer calories to operate.

The human body is genetically programmed to fight weight loss because starvation has long been a great threat to survival for humans. In fact, weight gain is a distinctly modern problem. Since your body can't tell the difference between dieting and starvation, it protects you by slowing down metabolism in order to become energy-efficient.

By the time someone has dieted and regained several times, he or she may have permanently altered his or her metabolism. So, even though he or she eats less during a diet, weight may not be lost, because calories are being burned more slowly.

Once caloric intake is cut down even more, the risk for other complications increases. With a very low caloric intake—at or below 800 calories a day—the body has to decide how it will spend those precious few calories. It will choose to feed vital organs, such as the brain, heart, and lungs, but it will be forced to forgo other functions. That's why someone on a very low-calorie diet often feels cold, dizzy, tired, or depressed. Hair may fall out, and nails will become brittle.

DIETING DOESN'T BRING HAPPINESS OR SUCCESS

Dieting restricts food and personal choice. Even if people lose weight on a diet, they often still feel deprived and like a failure. Even when weight loss occurs, lost pounds seldom address the real problems or personal issues of most dieters. Losing weight solves few, if any, emotional problems. Losing weight will not magically make dreams come true: a boyfriend won't suddenly appear; you still may not make the team; your divorced parents won't suddenly get back together.

Diets are not a solution to life's challenges. Losing weight seldom changes a person's life dramatically.

DIETING CAN LEAD TO EATING DISORDERS

Over one million Americans have an eating disorder. Between 5 and 20 percent will eventually die from medical complications resulting from their eating disorder. The three main types of eating disorders—anorexia nervosa, bulimia, and compulsive overeating—are usually related to emotional problems.

These three eating disorders are related in other ways. All share characteristics of food and eating obsessions. People with eating disorders use food as an escape from dealing with life's problems. Furthermore, many people with eating disorders alternate between anorexia nervosa, bulimia, and compulsive overeating. Experts have found that frequent dieters who severely restrict their food intake will also binge and purge to keep their weight off.

Experts don't know the exact causes of why some people develop an eating disorder. They do know that eating disorders generally start with a weight-loss diet. The diet usually is started just before or after:

- A major life change—like going to a new school, the onset of puberty, the birth of a sister or brother, a death in the family, or moving to a new city or town

- Serious family problems—such as drug or alcohol abuse by a family member, divorce, constant family fighting
- A trauma—such as sexual, physical, or verbal abuse.

Eating disorders are more than just food problems. They affect every aspect of a person's life: school, work, hobbies and interests, family life, friends, emotions, growth, and health. Eating issues consume someone with an eating disorder. The person's whole life gets swallowed by eating problems and their consequences.

Often, people with eating disorders view fasting, bingeing and purging, or compulsive exercising as solutions to their problems. They try to control their bodies by denying themselves food when they feel that they can't control what is happening around them. If you feel that many things in life are simply beyond your ability to control—if you aren't allowed to make decisions for yourself, if you have lost a parent or a loved one, if you are experiencing confusion in a relationship, or if you have been the victim of physical, verbal, or sexual abuse—you may turn to dieting and other obsessive weight behaviors as a way to assert control in your life.

Controlling parents can feed into developing an eating disorder as well. Sometimes parents may directly criticize you for what you look like or how much you eat. This may be intended as concern for your social life or goals, but it often does more harm than good. The message comes across that you're not good enough the way you are. These kinds of negative comments can set up a battlefield mentality between you and your parents. By commenting on your food intake, your parents come across as criticizing or even controlling you. And you may respond by purposely overeating in order to defy them. Another reaction is to fall into anorexic patterns of starvation, thinking that being thinner will somehow bring approval or attention from thin-conscious parents. But both of these reactions are unhealthy ways to cope with the problem.

And current research shows that more and more males—adults, teens, and children—are being diagnosed with eating disorders.

Anorexia Nervosa

"It was an obsession," said Kim, a nineteen-year-old who had struggled with anorexia. "What I used to do at dinnertime was arrange the little food I had on my plate according to color and size, and then I would create a mental picture of what it looked like in my stomach. And when I thought the inside of my stomach looked the way it should, I stopped eating. It was all about control. I'd eat maybe three baby carrots, six or eight peas, and a piece of steamed yellow squash—orange, green, and yellow—and then I'd picture them sitting there nicely arranged and uncrowded in my stomach.

PEOPLE WITH ANOREXIA MAY:

- Eat tiny portions, refuse to eat, or deny that they are hungry.
- Have abnormal weight loss or lose a large amount of weight in a short amount of time.
- Be hyperactive, depressed, moody, and insecure.
- Have an intense fear of being overweight or gaining weight.
- See themselves as fat no matter how thin they are. Such a distorted body image can result in, or be the result of, low self-esteem.
- Continue to lose weight, even if they are already very thin.
- Exercise constantly and excessively, especially in the early stages of anorexia. Often, they exercise to exhaustion.
- Complain of nausea or bloating after eating normal amounts of food.

- Binge eat, then purge. Purging is often done by vomiting or by using laxatives or diuretics.
- Avoid eating in front of family members or other people.
- Be obsessed with information about food, nutrition information, and good/bad foods. They often have unusual food rituals or food choices.
- Be proud of their low weight and discipline to stay underweight.
- Be highly self-controlled.
- Have a decrease in sexual drive or interest.

When no one was looking, I would slip the rest of the food off my plate to my dog. Thank goodness I don't do that anymore. It wasn't just silly; it was dangerous. I had no idea how I looked—I weighed eighty-four pounds, looked like a stick, and had no energy for anything. I'm much happier eating like a regular person now. But my dog," she laughed, "hasn't quite gotten over it yet!"

Kim was lucky to have confronted her anorexia before something terrible happened. People with anorexia nervosa (or *anorexia*), sometimes called the starvation sickness, refuse food because of a fear of being overweight. In the early stages of the disease, anorexics actually are hungry. They don't lose their appetite. But they refuse to eat enough to maintain a healthy weight. According to Frances M. Berg, editor of *Healthy Weight Journal,* about one in 500 teens develops anorexia. Most are female teens.

Denial of a low-weight problem and starving the body are what characterize people with anorexia. Anorexics are obsessed with food, weight, and being thin. Their obsessions cause them to deny their hunger. They refuse to eat or eat so little that they begin to starve themselves. And as they starve themselves to death, anorexics still see themselves as fat. Because they eat too few calories for their basic needs, their bodies slowly waste away. They don't get the life-sustaining nutrients they need for normal body functions and growth.

CONSEQUENCES OF ANOREXIA

Early Stages of Anorexia

- Dry, thinning hair on head
- Brittle nails
- Dull, sometimes yellowish, skin
- Constipation
- Dizziness
- Irregular or no menstrual periods because of hormonal imbalances

Later Stages of Anorexia

- Muscle cramps.
- Jumpy heart or irregular heartbeat.
- Body temperature drops below normal. Intolerance to cold weather. Cold or numb hands and feet, which may turn blue as a result.
- Sleep problems.
- Slow breathing or shortness of breath.
- Kidney problems.
- Memory loss and poor concentration.
- Exhaustion, weakness.
- Slow reflexes.
- Thin, fine body hair develops on arms, legs, and other body parts.
- Gaunt, skeletal look; sunken eyes. Loss of muscle and body fat.
- Stunted growth.
- Bone fractures.
- Death.

In the early stages of anorexia, most people are extremely hungry. They think about food and eating constantly. Yet they refuse to nourish their bodies with the right amounts and kinds of food. To compensate for the lack of nutrients and energy, the body stops dealing with functions that aren't vital for survival. Instead it marshals all available nutrients to keep the heart and other vital organs going. A starving body cuts off nutrients that go to the hair, nails, and skin. Females stop getting their menstrual periods. In the later stages of anorexia, people feel exhausted and lose interest in eating and food. Kidney problems, memory loss, and concentration problems arise.

There are plenty of unseen dangers that occur as the anorexic enters into the later stages of the disorder: smaller heart, brittle bones from mineral loss, very low blood pressure, and stunted growth. Fuzzy, downlike hair may grow on the arms, back, and other places. This hair, called lanugo, grows to help keep in body heat.

Bulimia

Like anorexics, people with bulimia are concerned with staying very thin. However, their methods of getting thin and staying thin differ from those with anorexia. Anorexics starve themselves by undereating or not eating. In contrast, bulimics eat food to make themselves feel better. But then they quickly get rid of it by purging. Purging means to get rid of food fast, often by vomiting or by using laxatives or diuretics.

The word *bulimia* is Greek. It means "ox

PEOPLE WITH BULIMIA MAY:

- Often eat secretly.
- Quickly go to the bathroom after eating, usually to purge.
- Quickly fluctuate in weight, although many are at a healthy weight or a little overweight.
- Eat huge meals or incredible amounts of snack food but not gain weight.
- Feel ashamed and depressed after bingeing.
- Abuse alcohol or take drugs.
- Become dependent on laxatives, diuretics, enemas, diet pills, or emetics to lose weight. *Emetics* are drugs or herbs that induce vomiting.
- Be overly concerned about their appearance, believing that they must be at an ideal weight at all times.
- Believe that vomiting or using laxatives is a way to diet.
- Feel out of control every time a binge-purge cycle occurs.

appetite" or "big appetite." Bulimia is more common than anorexia. According to Frances M. Berg, bulimia affects 1 to 3 percent of teens.

Bulimia is marked by binge-eating and purging cycles:

- *Bingeing* is when the person gulps down large amounts of food very fast. Often the food is high in calories, fat, and/or sugar. After a binge, the person feels guilty about all the excess calories and food consumed. The guilt leads to purging.
- *Purging* is when the person gets rid of the food quickly. The most common way to purge is by self-induced vomiting. Other people use laxatives to increase bowel movements, or diuretics to increase urine production.

Over time the bingeing and purging cycles increase. Or the person may routinely purge even if a small amount of food is eaten.

Bingers aren't hungry. Instead they are depressed, angry, upset, or anxious about something. They use food to deal with their emotions. Many times they don't really care what they eat, just as long as they're eating. Bingers eat fast, seldom really tasting or enjoying the food. They also can't stop until all the food is gone, even if they feel sick from all the food they have devoured.

Bulimics vary in how often they purge. But

purging just once a week can cause the body harm. Continued purging can seriously damage the body.

Vomiting is the most common method of purging. Stomach acids, as they move from the stomach to the throat and mouth, can eat away these body parts as well as the teeth and gums. Some bulimics have red, swollen cheeks. That is because the vomit can infect the salivary glands. Blood vessels in the cheeks can break, and sometimes the stomach ruptures. To induce vomiting, people may take ipecac, a nonprescription drug. When taken in large amounts, ipecac weakens the heart and damages the digestive system. Ipecac is used to induce vomiting if someone has eaten a poison.

People who purge may use laxatives to help them move their bowels. Continual use of laxatives can damage the digestive system. Continued abuse of laxatives causes bloating. Bulimics think that they are heavier than they are because of the uncomfortable feeling of being bloated. Some purgers develop a tolerance to laxatives. That means they need more and more of the drug to have a bowel movement. The usual dose of a laxative is one or two tablets a day. To have a bowel movement, laxative abusers sometimes need to take up to sixty tablets a day.

Compulsive Overeating

"I eat because food quiets me down," Linda said. "It makes me feel . . . less anxious. And sure, I know I eat more than I need to. No one has to tell me that. I've got all these extra pounds to remind me."

DANGERS OF PURGING

From Using Laxatives

- Stomach cramping, bloating, pain.
- Nausea.
- Gas.
- Constipation.
- Diarrhea.
- Dehydration.
- Causes essential nutrients to be poorly absorbed.
- Irregular heartbeat.
- Damages the colon so that it no longer functions. Removal of the colon may result.
- Tolerance to laxatives develops.

From Vomiting

- Damages throat, mouth, gums.
- Teeth become sensitive to heat and cold and develop spaces between them. Fillings can fall out. Damages tooth enamel and ultimately destroys teeth.
- Infection of the salivary glands. Swollen cheeks result.
- Stomach can rupture.
- Blood vessels in the cheeks can break.

From Using Diuretics

- Kidney damage
- Dehydration
- Irregular heartbeat

CONSEQUENCES OF BULIMIA

- Finger sores on hand (from inducing vomiting)
- Vomiting blood
- Tooth decay
- Swollen jaw or cheeks, swollen glands in neck
- Blurred vision
- Dry, flaky skin
- Broken blood vessels in face
- Irregular or no menstrual periods
- Weakness
- Mood swings, depression, isolation from friends and family, low self-esteem
- Fatigue
- Stomach pain, cramps, gas, bloating
- Sore throat
- Upset stomach
- Constipation, diarrhea
- Dehydration
- Stunted growth
- Bone fractures
- Kidney, liver damage
- Imbalance of body's minerals and fluids, resulting in heart attack
- Death

Linda paused. "But when I really think about it, I guess I use food kind of like the way people used to load cannons. You know, with that plunger thing? I just stuff down food in order to stuff down my feelings. When I feel sad or anxious or lonely, if I can stuff food down, then I don't have to deal with all that. The feelings stay down because the food is stuffed down on top of them."

Overeating, or compulsive eating, is the most common of the three eating disorders among teens and adults. There are many types of compulsive eaters. Some people learned to always overeat because their parents encouraged them to. Others overeat to deal with major stress or trauma, such as abuse or the death of a relative. Another kind of overeater is one who has set up rigid daytime rules about eating. He or she may eat very little for breakfast and lunch but binge alone after a full meal during the evening.

Another type of compulsive overeater is one who begins overeating because her parents constantly restrict her foods. As they keep warning her not to get fat and obsess over each mouthful of food she eats, her reaction is to rebel. And as a result, she becomes an overeater.

Tonya overeats when she's bored. "I'm home by myself for most of the evening. My mom is a single parent. She's a waitress at a small family restaurant and often doesn't get home until nine or ten. After I eat my evening meal, do the dishes, and then do my homework, I usually watch television until Mom gets home. I start out with a few cookies or a handful of chips to snack on. I'm always amazed, though, at how fast I go through so many boxes or bags of cookies or chips during those TV shows."

Like anorexics and bulimics, people who regularly overeat are behaving compulsively. Compulsive people are driven by a compelling desire to do a specific action in a certain way. Almost any activity can turn into a compulsion, including exercising, shopping, or overeating.

Compulsive behavior is actually a symptom of other problems. By doing something compulsively, people can hide their worries, fears, emptiness, or pain and instead focus on the compulsion. When things go well, some compulsive overeaters reward themselves by bingeing. No matter what triggers compulsive overeating, the person is left feeling ashamed, embarrassed, and lonely.

People who eat compulsively binge, often like a bulimic. Or they may nibble and snack, consuming large amounts of food over several hours. They are often overweight or obese. Compulsive overeaters generally won't overeat in front of other people, because they try to hide their behaviors. Unlike bulimics, compulsive overeaters won't purge or use drugs to remove excess food.

Like the other eating disorders, anorexia and bulimia, compulsive overeating can greatly harm the body.

CONSEQUENCES OF COMPULSIVE OVEREATING

- Obesity
- High blood pressure
- Hormone imbalances
- Raised cholesterol levels
- Overexertion/exhaustion
- Irregular heartbeat
- Poor circulation
- Decreased endurance
- Nutritional imbalances
- Mood swings, depression, isolation from friends and family, low self-esteem
- Joint pain
- Stomach pain, cramps, gas, bloating
- Constipation, diarrhea
- Decreased mobility

Eating disorders can be a major health threat. Getting help is essential. There are many treatments for various eating disorders and numerous organizations that offer support.

7 What's Right for Me?

If dieting to be thin isn't in, what's right for you? A healthier approach to looking and feeling good is to concentrate on being fit rather than on being thin. In fact, as long as our society values people based on how they look, dieting and its problems and consequences will continue to be a problem for many people.

Yet not all of us are meant to be slender, small, or wear tiny clothing sizes. We come in many sizes and shapes. You, your family members, and your friends may be tall or short, stocky or lanky, muscular or not. Because everyone differs, there's no such thing as a perfect body or an ideal body weight, shape, or size that will fit each person.

Being fit is the total package of your physical, mental, and social health. Whatever your shape and size today, you can choose a healthy lifestyle, one in which you:

- ⊙ Are physically active
- ⊙ Strive for a healthy weight

- Make reasonable choices for good health
- Choose a healthy eating style
- Make your goal overall body fitness rather than focusing on an unreachable perfect weight or body shape

WHAT'S A HEALTHY WEIGHT?

Question:
Won't the bathroom scale tell me if I'm at a healthy weight?

Answer:
No. Comparing your height and weight to a chart won't tell you if you are at a healthy weight. Your healthy weight is one that is right for you. It may differ from that for another person even if that person is the same height, age, and sex as you.

Your body weight is determined by many factors:

- Inherited genes that determine your health, size, and body-frame shape.
- Metabolic rate, or the rate at which your body burns energy.
- Body composition. Muscle burns more calories than body fat does.
- Level of physical activity.
- What you eat.
- Where your body fat is located.

- How much of your weight is fat.
- Whether you have weight-related health problems.

So you see, many factors can help determine healthy weight, so experts have developed several methods. Some use modified height-weight charts. However, these may not work well for teens who tend to gain weight and then appear to lose it during a growth spurt. Other experts focus on the ratio of fat to muscle, or body-mass index (BMI).

Another way of defining a healthy weight is in terms of waist-to-hip ratio. The idea here is that excess weight above the waist is not as healthy as excess weight below the waist. So people with weight above the waist—abdominal fat—are called apple shaped. People with excess weight on the hips or thighs are called pear shaped. Apples tend to be at greater risk than pears for certain health problems such as heart disease and diabetes.

EMOTIONAL SUPPORT GROUPS: TOPS, OA

Rather than help people lose weight, some commercial programs help people deal with their emotions. Two of the best-known low- or no-cost programs are Take Off Pounds Sensibly (TOPS) and Overeaters Anonymous (OA). These organizations offer support for a lifelong problem. They also provide a social network for people who feel alone with their problems.

TOPS

In 1948 Mrs. Esther Manz, a mother of five children, went to see her doctor. While in the waiting room, she flipped through magazines. An article on Alcoholics Anonymous (AA) caught her attention. The idea of people talking together and emotionally supporting each other appealed to her. Manz told her doctor about the concept of encouraging people to lose weight. He too liked the idea.

Manz soon invited three overweight friends to her Milwaukee, Wisconsin, home. She explained the basic idea: The four of them would talk and encourage each other to lose weight. They would meet weekly, over coffee. All agreed to her plan. By the second group meeting, the four women had lost a combined total of twenty-eight pounds. After a year, all had continued to lose weight.

Manz realized that she had found a marketable idea. As chair of the local PTA and a natural organizer, she found other people to join the group. Chapters began across the United States, each with its own name like Zipper Rippers, Button Busters, Tops Not Tubs, and so on. Manz wrote a manual to explain how and why TOPS worked.

Over time Manz added various incentives. Members now must weigh in before each meeting. Those who lose weight are treated like royalty. Those who lose a lot of weight are crowned kings or queens in special ceremonies. The TOPS system of praise and withdrawal of praise has been widely copied or adapted by various weight-loss groups. TOPS was the first organization to successfully use praise for weight loss.

TOPS does not sell or endorse diet products. Manz does not receive a salary through TOPS. Today there are about 12,000 chapters in the United States and Canada. As a nonprofit organization, TOPS donates any money left over from the small annual and weekly dues of its members for obesity research.

Overeaters Anonymous (OA)

Joan S. took a deep breath. She had never gone to a meeting like this before. "Hi. My name is Joan, and I'm a compulsive overeater. I used to eat six candy bars and five bags of potato chips, and then I'd eat a quart or two of ice cream. And that was after a full meal. I always had candy and snacks hidden under my bed."

Another woman spoke next. She had been a member of OA for a few months. "I'd eat three or four big servings of lasagna with a dozen breadsticks and a salad swimming in dressing. Then I'd decide if I was ***hungry****! I've been on so many diets. I've tried weight-loss patches and herbal teas and laxatives and hypnosis. At least coming to OA helps me to know I'm not alone in my compulsion to overeat."*

Such confessions are the core of each meeting of Overeaters Anonymous. OA is a fellowship of some 150,000 members worldwide. A housewife in Los Angeles, California, known only as Roxanne S., started OA in 1960. Roxanne S. and several other women with eating problems met in a suburban Los Angeles home. They decided to apply the twelve-step principles of AA to eating and weight control. OA's basic beliefs are:

- Obesity is caused by extreme psychological problems.
- Because compulsive overeating is an addiction, it is a chronic illness that can be arrested but not cured.
- Compulsive overeaters are people whose eating habits have caused continuing problems in their lives and for whom food has become an unmanageable problem.

Anonymity is key to OA. Like Joan S., most members usually give only their first names and sometimes their last initial. OA members are not to use last names when dealing with the media. Anonymity also means that information shared at meetings is to be held in confidence.

OA does not take a position on what members should or should not eat. It doesn't endorse any weight-loss program, plan, or product. OA is non-profit and charges no dues or fees. However, most groups do pass a basket or container to cover rent for the meeting place, OA literature, and coffee. OA has tools of recovery or methods to help members. These tools include abstinence, or refraining from compulsive eating. People work toward or maintain this abstinence by using the twelve steps. Similar to AA's twelve steps, OA's are a list of suggestions that help people live without the need for overeating. Here are some of the steps:

- Admitting that you are powerless over food
- Turning your will and your life over to the care of a power greater than yourself
- Making amends to people you have harmed as a result of your compulsive eating
- Trying to help other compulsive overeaters

Meetings are held on a continual basis. They last from one to two hours. OA holds various types of meetings, including:

- Meetings for beginners, although all meetings welcome newcomers.
- Step meetings. During step meetings, members focus on one of the twelve steps. They take turns sharing how they relate to that step.
- Discussion or pitch meetings, which are the majority of OA meetings. Here a leader shares for about ten minutes his or her story of compulsive overeating and recovery. People then raise their hands or go around the room taking turns talking about their problems or successes. Most people state first that they are compulsive overeaters. At some meetings, the group applauds

after people talk. Other groups time speakers so that no one person talks too much.

Almost all meetings start with a prayer called the serenity prayer. Meetings usually close with a prayer as well. People don't have to talk at meetings if they don't want to. Some members attend meetings twice a month, whereas others go to three or more meetings a week.

OA meetings are held worldwide in forty-seven countries. In the United States, meetings are held in all kinds of places: community buildings, churches, hospitals, and so on. OA's purpose is to help people stop eating compulsively. Weight loss may or may not result. The only requirement for membership is a desire to stop compulsive overeating. You don't even have to be overweight. In fact, thin or normal-weight people with anorexia nervosa or bulimia can join. Children who eat compulsively are welcome too, and there are groups just for teens.

COMBATING WEIGHT-LOSS FRAUD

The federal government and state governments have long battled weight-loss fraud. You can also learn how to spot and avoid weight-loss fraud.

The Government's Ongoing Battles

If so many weight-loss drugs, products, and gadgets are fake, why hasn't the government stopped their sales? One reason is that manufacturers are skilled at skirting FDA and FTC rules. They won't make a direct weight-loss claim. Instead they use a product name that makes people **believe** they will lose weight, such as EZ Slim, Fat Burner, PhytoSlim, Power Thin, Herbal Burners, NutraSlim and so on.

Some companies go further. They ignore the government rules and advertise their diet wares on television, in ad blitzes, and with toll-free telephone marketing schemes. They make lots of quick money, then go out of business when disappointed customers begin demanding their money back. The government can do little about this type of fraud.

Also, under the 1994 Dietary Supplements Health and Education Act, the FDA has little power to control and regulate the herbal and dietary supplements industry. Under this law:

- Herbal and dietary supplements are considered foods, not drugs.

- Food products don't have to meet the same level of safety and effectiveness as prescription or OTC (over-the-counter) drugs. This means that the FDA must ***prove*** that herbal and dietary supplements are unsafe. If these are proved unsafe, the FDA can stop sales and pull the product from store shelves.

- The FDA can't regulate herbal and dietary supplements. This means that buyers generally don't know how much of each ingredient they are actually getting in a supplement.

To prove that a product is unsafe requires that the FDA run a long and extremely costly investigation. The FDA has not received any extra money or people to investigate potentially harmful weight-loss products. Its authority is limited. So this agency can do little to limit the sales of fake diet supplements in health food stores or through magazines, newspapers, or the Internet.

The Dietary Supplements Act also gave manufacturers another legal advertising avenue. Although weight-loss products can't make claims on their labels, they are allowed to put product literature nearby. That is why you will see booklets, flyers, and other paper literature near weight-loss products. This literature suggests, without actually saying so, that herbs or other ingredients in products will help people lose weight.

Here's an example of a claim: "Thermogenic herbs direct the flow of blood away from the stomach, which diminishes hunger sensations." Claims like this are worded so that readers believe the product helps promote weight loss.

Looking at the Headlines—and Beyond

Newspapers, magazines, and other media sources often publish legitimate weight-loss news. But because the news media can find and publish information so quickly, sometimes health experts haven't reviewed and interpreted the findings. Here are some suggestions to help you understand weight-loss information that is communicated through media sources:

- Read the headline *and* the full article or news brief. Headlines are meant to grab the reader's attention. Sometimes they create a different impression when compared to what's actually in the article.

- The results of one study are just that—the results of *one* study. Until repeated scientific studies are carried out, each done in a systematic way, one study alone is not considered proof.
- Preliminary findings are only preliminary. More research and evidence are needed.
- Animal studies are sometimes the first step when researching a new weight-loss product. However, the results from animal studies may not apply to people.
- A well-conducted scientific study includes a large group of people. Long-term studies are more likely to produce valid results.
- Check for particular words in the article or report, such as "suggest," "prove," "linked to," and "causes." In scientific and medical research, each of these terms means something different. Credible professionals are careful not to mislead people with these words.
- Responsible scientists and other health professionals don't claim proof

or cause unless repeated studies show that the findings are conclusive.

- Numbers can be either important or meaningless. For example, "increases the risk" and "lowers the risk" are phrases sometimes used in study findings, media reports and articles, or ads. Unless the risk is also stated, these phrases are useless. Also, if the risk was one in one million, and one study claims that a risk was doubled, that's still only one in 500,000. That may not mean much. On the other hand, if the risk was one in 100, and it doubles, that's a big increase.

- If a scientific or medical result is statistically significant, this means that the association between two factors is greater than what might occur at random. Statistical significance is worked out by a mathematical formula. However, people sometimes see the word "significant" and think it means "major" or "important." It may not.

Print and Electronic Misinformation

Some diet books and magazines as well as electronic sources can offer good, safe advice and suggestions on healthy weight. But diet or weight information is not necessarily accurate or reliable just because it is printed in a book, magazine, or newsletter; hyped on television or radio; or posted on the Internet. Some sources are totally inaccurate. Others may have threads of truth but contain plenty of misinformation. Still others really are reliable.

FINDING RELIABLE WEIGHT-LOSS HELP

Nutrition, weight management, and healthy eating information is provided throughout the United States by many health, education, and social service organizations as well as by individuals in private practice. To find a qualified nutrition expert or to get reliable answers to nutrition and healthy eating questions, contact:

- Your local doctor, clinic, health maintenance organization (HMO), or hospital for a referral.
- Your local dietetic association, public health department, extension service, or the nutrition department of a nearby college or university.
- The toll-free Consumer Nutrition Hot-Line of the American Dietetic Association's National Center for Nutrition and Dietetics at (800) 366-1655. Ask for a referral to a registered dietitian (RD) in your area.

Who's a Qualified Nutrition Expert?

Sometimes it's tough to determine whether someone is truly a nutrition, diet, or health expert. Qualified experts have specific academic and training credentials. Their degrees:

- Are in nutrition, dietetics, public health, or related fields such as biochemistry or medicine. They might also have a nutrition specialty in family and consumer sciences.
- Come from accredited colleges and universities. To find out whether a university or college is accredited, ask a reference librarian at a local public library.

It may seem like alphabet soup, but the initials after a qualified nutrition or health expert's name mean something. But beware: Even if a person has academic degrees, nutrition may not be his or her specialty.

Here are some degrees that really mean something:

RD, for Registered Dietitian

An RD is a reliable authority on the role of food and nutrition in health. To earn an RD, a person must successfully complete:

- A four-year degree in nutrition or a related field from an accredited college or university that is approved by the American Dietetic Association
- A supervised internship program

- An exam administered by the Commission on Dietetic Registration, which is the credential agency of the American Dietetic Association

To stay current, RDs must complete seventy-five or more hours of continuing education every five years.

DTR, for Dietetic Technician, Registered

A DTR is a reliable authority on the role of food and nutrition in health. To earn a DTR, a person must successfully complete:

- At least an associate degree from an accredited college or university
- A 450-hour dietetics program approved by the American Dietetic Association
- An exam administered by the Commission on Dietetic Registration, which is the credential agency of the American Dietetic Association

To stay current, DTRs must complete fifty or more hours of continuing education every five years.

Watch Out for These People

Two titles to watch out for are *nutritionist* and *diet counselor*. Many states don't regulate nutritionists or diet counselors. So people with these titles may or may not be nutrition experts.

Other groups of people to watch out for are salespeople for dietary supplements, so-called health advisors, and some authors who call themselves nutritionists. Many have decided that they are experts but in reality are not. Some may have a little nutrition training. Others may have mail-order credentials.

Mail-order credentials may come from a "diploma mill." The U.S. Department of Education defines a diploma mill as an organization awarding degrees without requiring its students to meet educational standards established and followed by reputable colleges and universities. To deal with diploma mill degrees, some states are licensing qualified nutrition experts. However, these laws are not in place everywhere, and qualifications differ for each state.

Is a Commercial Weight-Loss Program or Support Group for You?

Some people on weight-loss programs do lose weight and maintain all or some of their weight loss. Others really like what support groups such as OA or TOPS offer. Why? Each person differs in motivation, skills, knowledge, or in other ways. To determine whether a particular weight-loss center or support group is right for you, ask yourself the following questions:

- Do you lack knowledge or understanding about food labels, food preparation, or nutrition?
- Do you need group support and encouragement?
- Do you need help keeping motivated?

- Do you enjoy structure?
- Do you need accountability?
- Do you lack the time to put a program together by yourself?

If you answered yes to most of these questions, a commercial program may be an option for you. These programs can offer group support, structure, accountability, and motivation. Be aware, though, of the poor long-term record of most of these programs. They also require your time, commitment, and some—or a lot—of your money.

AND THE WINNER IS—YOU!

There is more to life than obsessing over food. Rather than living in a state of constant self-denial and dieting, aim instead for a healthy, happy lifestyle—one that fits who you really are.

GUIDELINES FOR SAFE WEIGHT LOSS

Don't diet or fast to lose weight

- Think of healthy eating as a long-term commitment.
- A healthy diet includes moderate amounts of a variety of foods and is high-fiber, low-fat, and enjoyable.

Avoid diet products

Don't use diet pills, laxatives, diuretics, or weight-loss herbs or supplements. Most are ineffective, and some are unsafe.

Reduce fat slightly

- Typical American diets run close to 40 percent fat. The American Heart Association, American Cancer Society, and many other professional health organizations recommend diets of no more than 30 percent fat.
- Don't eliminate all fat from your diet. Consuming no fat can lead to health problems.

Lose no more than one pound per week

The old recommendation of two pounds a week as a sensible weight-loss goal is currently considered too fast for long-term, healthy weight management.

Be physically active

- ⊙ Exercise can mean the difference between a successful, healthy weight program and one that fails.
- ⊙ Exercise helps the body burn more calories and speeds up the metabolism.
- ⊙ Recommendation: Exercise thirty minutes a day, three times a week.

Choose foods from all five groups in the food pyramid

- ⊙ 6—11 servings of bread and grains
- ⊙ 3—5 servings of vegetables
- ⊙ 2—4 servings of fruit
- ⊙ 2—3 servings of milk products
- ⊙ 2—3 servings of meat, poultry, fish, eggs, and beans
- ⊙ Small amounts of fat and sugar

Listen to your internal signals

Dieters often eat because of external cues, like "the clock says it's noon and time for lunch," or "that cherry pie looks good."

Instead of reacting to external cues, eat only when you are really hungry.

Have an occasional treat

When you want some chocolate, eat a little! But enjoy fatty or sugary treats in moderation.

Turn off the television

- Experts say that teens watch more than twenty hours of television each week. Often, they snack on high-fat foods while watching.
- Enjoy a few favorite TV shows, but avoid being a couch potato!

Crisis or problem? Avoid raiding the refrigerator or scarfing down cookies or chips.

Don't use food to cope with a problem or crisis. Instead, figure out what frustrations trigger you to use food as a crutch. Then develop new coping strategies such as going for a walk, listening to your favorite music, playing with your dog or cat, or talking to a friend.

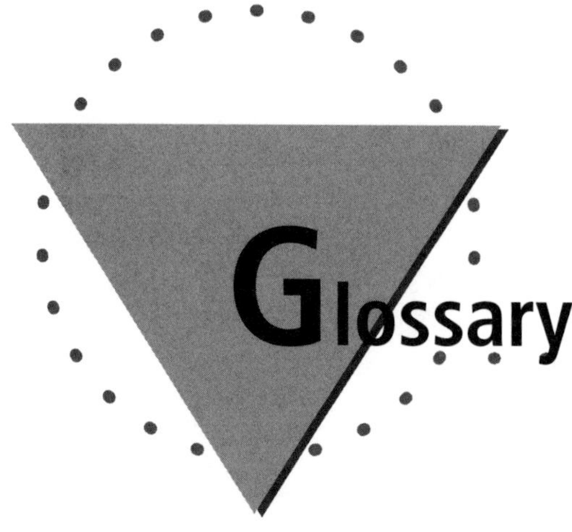

Glossary

Amphetamines Stimulants that speed up the heart and breathing; can cause anxiety, sleeplessness, and loss of appetite.

Anorexia nervosa An eating disorder characterized by self-starvation and brought on by psychological problems.

Binge Rapid, uncontrolled eating of large amounts of food.

Binge-purge syndrome A condition in which a person eats a large amount of food in a short period of time and then vomits to get rid of it.

Bulimia nervosa An eating disorder characterized by bingeing and purging.

Carbohydrates Sugars, starches, and fiber, which are the body's preferred source of energy.

Compulsion An urgent, repeated behavior.

Consequence The result of an action.

Crisis An extreme change in a person's life.

Diuretic A drug that increases the flow of urine.

Eating disorder An unhealthy way of dealing with food.

Elimination The expulsion of undigested food or body waste.

Enamel The hard material that covers the crown of the tooth; can be worn away as a result of frequent vomiting.

Fatigue Extreme tiredness that lowers one's level of activity.

Ipecac A syrup used to induce vomiting.

Laxative A drug used to induce a bowel movement.

Metabolism The rate at which the body burns food.

Nutrients Substances, such as vitamins, found in food and which the body needs to function properly.

Obesity A state of weighing 30 percent more than the standard weight for one's height.

Overeating An eating disorder characterized by the frequent eating of much larger quantities of food than needed to simply satisfy hunger.

Nonprescription Drugs sold over-the-counter without a doctor's written instructions or consent.

Prescription Drugs obtained exclusively by a doctor's written instructions and through a pharmacy.

Purge Elimination of food through self-induced vomiting, laxatives, diuretics, or fasting.

Stimulant A drug that increases the action of the central nervous system, heart, respiratory rates, and blood pressure, and causes the pupils to dilate and the appetite to decrease.

Testimonial An individual's personal recommendation of a product.

Underweight Being 10 to 15 percent below the standard weight for one's height.

Where to Go for Help

EATING DISORDER INFORMATION

Many organizations exist to help people who have eating disorders. These places can locate a therapist or counselor, provide information, or help during a crisis.

Academy for Eating Disorders (AED)
Montefiore Medical School
Department of Adolescent Medicine
111 East 210th Street
Bronx, NY 10467
(718) 920-6782

American Academy of Pediatrics (AAP)
P.O. Box 747
Elk Grove Village, IL 60009-0747
(708) 228-5005
Web site: http://www.aap.org/

American Anorexia/Bulimia Association (AABA)
165 West 46th Street, #1108
New York, NY 10036
(212) 575-6200
Web site: http://members.aol.com/amanbu/

American Eating Disorder Center
330 West 58th Street
New York, NY 10019
(212) 582-5190

Anorexia Nervosa and Bulimia Association (ANAB)
767 Bayridge Drive
P.O. Box 20058
Kingston, Ontario K7P 1C0
(613) 547-3684
Web site: http://www.ams.queensu.ca/anab

Anorexia Nervosa and Related Eating Disorders, Inc. (ANRED)
P.O. Box 5102
Eugene, OR 97405
(541) 344-1144
Web site: http://www.anred.com

Center for the Study of Anorexia and Bulimia
1 West 91st Street
New York, NY 10024
(212) 595-3449

Eating Disorders Awareness and Prevention (EDAP)
603 Stewart Street, #803
Seattle, WA 98101
(206) 386-3587
Web site: http://members.aol.com/edapinc/home.html

National Association of Anorexia Nervosa and Associated Disorders (ANAD)
P.O. Box 7
Highland Park, IL 60035
(847) 831-3438
Web site: http://www.medpatients.com/

National Association to Advance Fat Acceptance, Inc. (NAAFA)
P.O. Box 188620
Sacramento, CA 95818
(916) 558-6880
Fax: (916) 558-6881
Web site: http://www.naafa.org/

National Eating Disorders Organization (NEDO)
6655 South Yale Avenue
Tulsa, OK 74136
(918) 481-4044
Web site: http://www.laureate.com/nedointro.html

National Institute of Mental Health Eating Disorders Program
Building 10, Room 35231
Bethesda, MD 20892
(301) 496-1891
Web site: http://www.nimh.nih.gov/

Overeaters Anonymous Headquarters (OA)
P.O. Box 44020
Rio Rancho, NM 87174
(505) 891-2664

Take Off Pounds Sensibly (TOPS)
4575 South Fifth Street
P.O. Box 07360
Milwaukee, WI 53207-0360
(414) 482-4620
(800) 932-8677
Web site: http://www.tops.org/

DIET AND NUTRITION INFORMATION

American College of Sports Medicine
P.O. Box 1440
Indianapolis, IN 6206-1440
(317) 637-9200
Fax: (317) 634-7817
Web site: http://www.acsm.org/sportsmed/index.htm

The American Council on Science and Health, Inc. (ACSH)
1995 Broadway, 2nd Floor
New York, NY 10023-5860
(212) 362-7044
Fax: (212) 362-4919
Web site: http://www.acsh.org/index.html

The American Dietetic Association
216 West Jackson Boulevard
Chicago, Illinois 60606-6995
(312) 899-0040
Fax: (312) 899-1979
Web site: http://www.eatright.org/

Center for Science in the Public Interest (CSPI)
1875 Connecticut Avenue NW, Suite 300
Washington, DC 20009-5728
(202) 332-9110
Fax: (202) 265-4954
Web site: http://www.cspinet.org/

The National Council Against Health Fraud, Inc.
P.O. Box 1276
Loma Linda, CA 92354-9983

(909) 824-4690
Fax: (909) 824-4838
Web site: http://www.ncahf.org/

Quackwatch, Inc.
A member of Consumer Federation of America
P.O. Box 1747
Allentown, PA 18105
(610) 437-1795
Web site: http://www.quackwatch.com/index.html

For Further Reading

Barrett, Stephen, and William T. Jarvis (eds.). *The Health Robbers: A Close Look at Quackery in America*. Buffalo, NY: Prometheus Books, 1993.

Berg, Frances M. "Afraid to Eat: Children and Teens in Weight Crisis." Hettinger, ND: *Healthy Weight Journal*, 1997.

Bode, Janet. *Food Fight: A Guide to Eating Disorders for Preteens and Their Parents*. New York: Simon & Schuster, 1997.

Epstein, Diane, and Kathleen Thompson. *Feeding on Dreams: Why America's Diet Industry Doesn't Work and What Will Work for You*. New York: Macmillan Publishing Co., 1994.

Federal Trade Commission, Bureau of Consumer Protection, Office of Consumer & Business Education. *Fraudulent Health Claims: Don't Be Fooled*. Washington, DC: 1996.

Federal Trade Commission, Bureau of Consumer Protection, Office of Consumer & Business Education. *The Skinny on Dieting*. Washington, DC: 1996.

Fraser, Laura. *Losing It: America's Obsession with Weight and the Industry That Feeds On It.* New York: Dutton, 1997.

Hesse-Biber, Sharlene Janice. *Am I Thin Enough Yet?: The Cult of Thinness and the Commercialization of Identity.* New York: Oxford University Press, 1996.

Patterson, Charles. *Eating Disorders.* Austin, TX: Raintree Steck-Vaughn, 1995.

Sirimarco, Elizabeth. *Eating Disorders.* New York: Marshall Cavendish, 1994.

Sonder, Ben. *Eating Disorders: When Food Turns Against You.* New York: Franklin Watts, 1993.

Spies, Karen Bornemann. *Everything You Need to Know About Diet Fads.* New York: Rosen Publishing Group, 1993.

Tufts University Health & Nutrition Letter (available at public libraries)]. P.O. Box 57857, Boulder, CO 80328

U.S. Department of Agriculture: *Nutrition and Your Health: Dietary Guidelines for Americans.* Washington, DC, 1995.

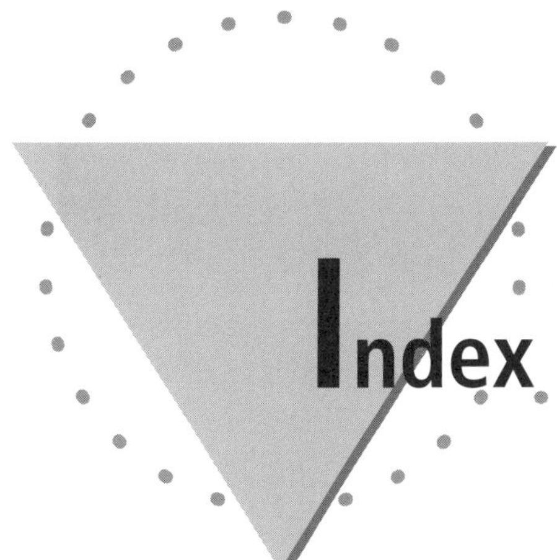

A

B

C

D